A Mystic's Way

A Mystic's Way

Mark Patterson

Writers Club Press
New York Lincoln Shanghai

A Mystic's Way

All Rights Reserved © 2003 by Mark Patterson

No part of this book may be reproduced or transmitted in any form or by any means, graphic, electronic, or mechanical, including photocopying, recording, taping, or by any information storage retrieval system, without the written permission of the publisher.

Writers Club Press
an imprint of iUniverse, Inc.

For information address:
iUniverse, Inc.
2021 Pine Lake Road, Suite 100
Lincoln, NE 68512
www.iuniverse.com

ISBN: 0-595-26909-5

Printed in the United States of America

Contents

CHAPTER 1	Things I'd Like Christianity to Answer	1
CHAPTER 2	What Happens When We Die?	4
CHAPTER 3	Seeing God Everywhere	12
CHAPTER 4	Messages From the Masters	30
CHAPTER 5	How do you start over when you feel have nothing to start from?	40
CHAPTER 6	God Believes in Me	47
CHAPTER 7	Life Scripting	53
CHAPTER 8	Religion's Dark Side	58
CHAPTER 9	Where was God on 9/11?	66
CHAPTER 10	What does God and our Angels want?	73
CHAPTER 11	Placing Spirituality back into our Sexuality Spiritual Orgasms	76
CHAPTER 12	What is your relationship with God?	81
CHAPTER 13	How can you ascend into Heaven if you keep nailing yourself to the Cross?	88
CHAPTER 14	The Violet Flame of Forgiveness	90
CHAPTER 15	That is just the story of my Life	95

1

Things I'd Like Christianity to Answer

For the life of me, I have never understood Christianity. I recall as a child, my father always wanted me to go to Church and profess Jesus as my savior. From the moment I walked into the Church doors, I absolutely knew that I did not want to be there. I knew that something simply did not feel right. Maybe it was due to the fact that I continually saw Angels around others and me as a child. Maybe it was due to the fact that I knew what people would think and feel before they did as a child. Maybe in my magical state of innocence in my trusting I knew that God was already within me. Some how, that inner knowing was replaced with insecurity, doubt, and fear as I grew up into my adolescence and teen years. I soon found myself burdened with tremendous guilt over taking things from my mother and grandmother and having to lie to them about it. I had deep feelings of shame around having an erection and my frequent urges to masturbate.

One night my guilt was so unbearable, that I found myself watching TV evangelist Pat Robertson who proclaimed, "Confess that you are a sinner, and allow Jesus to come into your heart, and deliver you from the bondage of guilt." Immediately, I turned off the TV and I went down on my knees and prayed to Jesus to come into my heart and deliver me from my deep seeded feelings of guilt and shame. I prayed to Jesus that no one find out that I have an erection every morning. I prayed to Jesus that I was not going to masturbate any more. I prayed that my mom and my grandmother forgive me for lying to them. I prayed that no one find out that I was attracted to girls. I prayed that Jesus come into my life and deliver me from the "chains of guilt" that kept me bounded to pain. I felt lonely so I went to bed early that night crying. Upon awakening in the following morning, I recalled my dreams being very vivid, as if the Angels of my childhood had returned to my side. They instructed me to flip through the Bible and to stop when I felt a "tingle" in my heart. So, I looked to the left of my headboard and picked up a Bible, my yearly Christmas present from my father, and I thumbed through the pages, and as the Angels said, there was a tingle in my heart so I stopped. I was in the book of John, and I read the words of Jesus; "Is it not written in your laws, I say yea are Gods?" I thought to myself, how can I be a "sinner" if Jesus says, "we are Gods?" Then I found myself in the book of Matthew were Jesus said; "Judge not that ye be Judged for the Judgment that you have will be the Judgment that you get, and the measure that you give will be the measure that you shall receive." Again, I thought, "doesn't this imply that we are not judged by God, but rather we are only judged to the extent that we Judge others?" Again, I continued to flip the pages of the Bible where I stopped upon the teachings of Jesus, "Be you *perfect* for the Kingdom of Heaven is within." Again I wondered, "If I am perfect, like he said, then am I really a sinner?" If the Kingdom of Heaven is within us, then why do I need to die, in order to experience it?" Then I came to a passage in the book of Genesis where it states; "The Son's of God saw that the wives of men were fair and decided to take them as their own. They came into them and bore children. These were men of great renowned and of great strength." I wondered, "How could Jesus be God's only son, when the book of Genesis it indicates something different?" I thought not only does it state that there is more than one Son of God; it also implies that they committed adultery. I continued my thumbing through and the sensations within my heart continued to spring up. Again, I stopped and read the words of Jesus, "Except yea be converted and become as little Children, you shall not enter the Kingdom of Heaven." I thought, "If Jesus is the light and the truth and the way, then how could becoming childlike open the door to God?"

Then I decided to set the Bible down and more questions began to pop into my inquisitive mind. I couldn't understand the idea that we were to be afraid of God. My mind continued to ponder why we were to be afraid of God's judgments upon us? I felt that God was love. In my adolescent mind, I felt that love was a good thing. Love was something that was wanted. Then I thought of all of the words that related to love; healing, compassion, forgiveness, joy, fulfillment, and peace. Yet, judgment was not one of them. In fact as far as I could tell, it is impossible for Love to render any kind of Judgment. Love simply cannot judge. I also wanted to know why is it that we know nothing of Jesus' life from the time that he was 12 to 30? What did he do in those 18 years? Surely, someone somewhere must have followed and recorded the single most important human life in the history of mankind? I also questioned his name. I mean if Jesus was Jewish, then why does he have a Puerto Rican name? My intuitive process also questioned his race. Were there any Caucasian people in the Middle East 2000 years ago? I also wondered if God made man in His image and His likeness, didn't this imply that we are God like? How can the Bible really be the word of God? There are so many fundamental things wrong with this concept. I mean, why are their four different stories about the resurrection? If it were really God's word, wouldn't there just be one story of the resurrection? Why are there two different stories on the birth of Jesus? I mean in the book of Mark, the three wise men brought gifts, and in the book of Luke, they just honored his birth without gifts. If we had been indoctrinated with the idea that we were to honor the birth of Jesus rather than bring gifts, would our Holidays be as crazy as they are? I asked to myself, "How can I be a sinner, born in sin, just for being here?" Why is it that there is a 600, year span of syntax and grammatical changes in the books of Peter and Paul? Why did God only talk to men? Why don't we have a gospel according to Mary or Jane? I woke up feeling more confused then ever before. I couldn't believe that I had watched Pat Robertson that TV evangelist who loves to say, "God has a message for you, send in those checks now." I wondered, "Did I really proclaim, Jesus as my savior?" Why? Well, these are questions that Christianity continued to avoid, were answered about a week later, when I had a Near Death Experience due to alcohol poisoning.

2

What Happens When We Die?

On February 1, 1986, I had a Near Death Experience (NDE). I was an irrational teenager who thought it would be really cool to consume vast amounts of alcohol. After two beers, four wine coolers and a fifth of vodka, my body went into cardiac arrest and I found myself in Heaven. Twenty-two minutes later, another soul came in and took the place of the original. In other words, I am a walk-in. However, something very unusual happened—the soul that took over after the original one left walked in from the future. Former NASA Physicist Barbara Ann Brennan writes in *Hands of Light*: "Future lifetimes can be placed in the auric field at birth and can be taken on at the completion of a lifetime if the individual so chooses." (Brennan, p. 262)

So, basically I reincarnated into the same body. I evolved five lifetimes with a fifth of vodka. (Please, do not try this at home, as you may not get the same results as I did.) As I lay unconscious on the bathroom floor of the Canterbury Suite in Coralville, Iowa, I began to hear an incredibly beautiful sound—a sound so healing that it was, and is, beyond description. My attention then switched to the fact that I was no longer in my body. I panicked. I called out to my classmates, who just an hour earlier were chanting, "go, go, go" as I was chugging down a fifth of vodka. My cries for help soon fell upon deaf ears. No one could see that I was dead; no one could see that I was no longer in my body. What was most terrifying was the fact that no one could hear me. The music from the celestial choir filled me with an overwhelming feeling of peace and love. My "vision" looked upward and I saw the gates of Heaven open before my eyes. There was an iridescent glowing light. It was as if I was being pulled by a magnetic force into the light. I was at complete peace—there was no pain, no sadness, just love. I also had this strange feeling that I existed on many different levels of reality at the same time. In an instant I felt a knowing of other times, other places, other worlds. I wondered if I was going to ever see my mother again? I wondered about my father, and my family? My longing for them soon left me as the echoes of essence were soon filled with curiosity.

Five angels then greeted me. They must have been 10 to 12 feet in height and they glowed with a bluish-white color. An absolute love radiated from them to me. I felt like I knew them and that I had known them before. It was if by telepathic thoughts they began to answer my inquisitive mind. "Yes, we know you, and you indeed know us." "We have been with you since your moment of birth and we were assigned to watch over you, protect you and guide you." "You have forgotten the magical closet of your childhood bedroom." "You have forgotten to listen to us." "You have forgotten that we even exist." "But we are here, always at your beckon call, ready to assist you on your journey." "For you are never alone." "We are you." We are you? I wondered?

Then they took me to a room with a table; the table was transparent and looked like a hologram. They proceeded to say, "This is your life." The table then turned into images of the life I had been living, and the dialogue between my angels and me went something like this:

Mark: "My father left me when I was three. He is pathetic; I hate him."

Angels: "How does that relate to love?"

Mark: "My mother, she is never around and never listens to me. I hate her, too."

Angels: "How does that relate to love?"

Mark: "There is my cousin, Shawn. Watch me kick his a**."

Angels: "How does that relate to love?"

Mark: "My neighbor is black. I don't like black people."

Angels: "How does that relate to love?"

Mark: "You see John over there? He is gay, an f**king faggot, homosexual."

Angels: "How does that relate to love?"

Mark: "Look at all of my classmates. They suck, f**k them all."

Angels: "How does that relate to love?"

Mark: "There is that TV evangelist telling me that I need to be saved. F**k that Jesus s**t."

Angels: "How does that relate to love?"

Mark: "Oh, you keep saying that. How does what relate to love?"

Angels: "Mark, everything in life is a test to see if you will respond with fear or love. You are not being judged here. However, there is one thing that you will be measured by—your ability to love unconditionally. When you learn to respond only with love, then you will evolve and thus end the cycle of karma and reincarnation.

"Jesus was sent to Earth to show people how to end the cycle of karma and reincarnation. This is done through compassion, forgiveness, and non-judgment. When you respond with hate, blame, fear and resentment, you create the same experiences over and over again, lifetime after lifetime. Eventually, you become what you most hate. Throughout your lifetimes, you will experience various roles—good, bad, rich, poor, victim and martyr. As you experience all things, you will realize there is nothing and no one to judge. When you let go of judgment, you will develop compassion for all life. Once you do that, the cycle of karma and reincarnation will end. By the looks of things, you are going to incarnate as a black, gay, overweight, TV evangelist in your next lifetime. Karma was never intended to be a punishment. It was given to humanity to ensure that each and every one of you would be held 100 percent responsible for your own life. That is why Jesus said, 'Do unto others as you would have them do unto to you.'"

Mark: "Lifetime after lifetime? I am going to come back as an overweight, gay, black male who preaches about Jesus? Wait a minute? How does that relate to love?"

Angels: "Yes, lifetime after lifetime. You call it reincarnation. You see Mark; you chose the parents that you *think* that you hate before you came here. You made agreements and contracts with them before you incarnated on Earth. Everything is already laid out for you. All things are predestined. The only thing you can control is how you respond to what happens to you. You chose a pattern that was set in the stars at the time of your conception, a path that would most help you evolve."

Doreen Virtue, Ph.D., writes the following in *The Light Workers Way*:

> Before your birth, you and a spiritual council of guides created a life plan tailored to meet your material, spiritual, and karmic needs. This Divine plan has three elements: a purpose, personal growth lessons, and relationships with other people to support the overall plan.
>
> Your purpose is a task you are to do through your career, volunteer work, or a special project that uses your natural talents and interests to benefit humanity. Your plan's second element entails well-timed life events that teach you about love and help you to shed self-defeating personality traits.

> The third element involves pre-birth arrangements you made with certain people who will serve as catalysts for your purpose and personal growth. These people may function as your family members, co-workers, friends, or acquaintances. Your interactions with these people simultaneously help them to fulfill their own plans.
>
> Your predestined plan is a rough outline of what your life would look like, including your purpose, significant life lessons, and relationships with particular people. Because the plan is only a rough outline, you must choose the finer details of your plan as you go through life. You are free to ignore the plan completely but the emotional and societal consequences of this choice can be devastating. (Virtue, p. 72)

Of course, you have forgotten all of this. The areas in life that you most struggle with are those where you have not yet learned self-mastery. You have forgotten to remember your natural state of love. Instead of demonstrating your self-mastery, you have demonstrated your fears.

Don't worry, you will have unlimited opportunities to demonstrate love. Love is what makes all things possible. Love is the answer. Love is who you are, be that love."

Mark: "What about God?"

Angels: "Go on."

Mark: "Does He exist?"

Angels: "Yes, She does!"

Mark: "She?" "Where do I find God?"

Angels: "God is within your heart.

The Kingdom of Heaven is found within your very being. Above all things seek the Kingdom of Heaven that is within you. Become it, be it, embrace it and discover that which is within you, loves you, adores you, wants you to succeed, and it believes in you. It believes in your dreams. It wants what you want. It believes in who you are. It believes in you."

Mark: "God believes in me?"

Angels: "God believes in you, and in time you will come to know the love that comes from within. God's love is within your heart. Until you accept the unconditional love that your inner being has for you, you will rely on the conditional love that comes from others. As you have not been taught about your inner unconditional love and total acceptance that your inner being has for you. Dear child, your inner being adores you, admires you, and longs for you to know of the love that it has for you. Rather than trusting its love, you have learned to rely and depend on outer love and outer acceptance. Because of your dependence on outer love, you feel insecure, filled with self-doubt. You have learned to allow others to determine your worthiness.

Mark, you have learned to become a martyr to your own joy. You have done this do get out of others what it is that you *think* that you want. You give out of the expectation that others will give back too you. You have become like an investment banker. How does this serve you? Shall we say, that you *demand* that others give back too you. Then when they don't, you become filled with resentment. In your self-imposed resentment, you get to be "right" that you are unworthy of receiving it. You unconsciously create outer relationships that are filled with conditions, and tests to each other. I doubt your love and my love so I need your proof, that you love me. You have to do this or be this, or act this way so I can be certain, sure of your love, and my love. My happiness and joy becomes dependent only when I can please you. THIS NEVER WORKS. The demands get larger and more challenging; it only leads to uncertainty and doubt. When one is certain and secure of their unconditional love of themselves, from themselves, there is no need for tests or for proof. Conditional love is never felt as love because it can never be given freely. Only unconditional love can be felt and experienced because it is free and no one is put through tests or made to perform like a circus monkey, to show and prove to someone they are fully loved and accepted." The Angels continued:

"If you feel that another does not honor you, respect you, or appreciate you, they are a reflection of how you do not honor, respect, or appreciate yourself. Life is your mirror. Learn to see yourself in other people. See yourself in all things. Yes, there will be challenges, hardships, and frustrations, as you seem to learn only through pain, but the potential rewards are equally as great. You are loved dear child."

Then the angels introduced me to a brilliant being. "He" had to be 20 feet tall and I felt an incredible love coming from him to me. The angels explained that I was going to go home to God now and that this being would take over for me and complete the rest of my physical life. They said that they would always be in my heart and not to forget them, that they loved me and that I was never alone. At that moment, my consciousness shifted from walking into a pristine place of peace to this brilliant being who was about to enter my body. In one breath, I was literally "slammed" into a completely unconscious body. The amount of energy that it takes to awaken a "dead" body is phenomenal. It was as if I had been struck by lightning.

My face lies in a pool of blood and vomit. My body and face had turned completely green. I could not breathe and passed out once again. Several hours later, my friends drove me home, as my mom was gone for the weekend. When I woke up, it was as if I had never been on Earth before. I felt very frightened, but then recalled who spoke to me while I was passed out the previous night. Merlin had visited me in my drunken state of oblivion and revealed a caste system that was the hierarchy of the Alpha and Omega Order of Melchizedek. (Yes, it is Merlin as in King Arthur and the Knights of the Round Table.) Did Merlin really come to me that night? Did he really describe the geometric caste system of the Melchizedek priesthood? Yes, I am now convinced of it. Why he did this is still unclear. But for now, I want to go back to the question that I was asked by my angels during my Near Death Experience: "How does that relate to love?"

I find it funny, this WWJD? "What would Jesus do?" Really, what would Jesus do? Do you really think that if Jesus were here, he would be out on corners asking people, "Are you saved?" Or telling them, "You need to be saved!" Do you think he would say, "AIDS is God's way of punishing those for being gay?" Or that he would condemn people for being gay or lesbian? Do you think he would condemn people who choose to be in an interracial marriage? Do you think he would suppress women as the Catholic Church has done? Would Jesus condone the Catholic Church's response to most wife beatings? Or divorce requests? Do you think that he would be pleased to see what the Catholic Church has done with his teachings? Do you think that he would be pleased to see the wealth of the Vatican and the majority of churches, and the poverty of their followers? Or that he would be pleased to see the TV Evangelist who makes 80 million dollars a year while proclaiming, "God has a message for you—send in those checks now!" Do you think that he would call Jews sinners who need to be converted? Do you think he would call upon the Islamic Fundamentalist to be saved? Do you really think that he would call anyone a sinner? Indeed, what would Jesus do? The question is not, "What would Jesus do?" The more profound question is, "What would LOVE do?"

When you are lying on your deathbed, you will not worry about the money, cars, or homes that you collected on the way. You will wonder about the relationship with your father that you did not heal. You will wonder about your spouse and remember how you refused to forgive him or her for what was done to you so many years ago. You will wonder if you loved your children enough. You will ask, "Why was I so angry?" You will wonder about the relationship with your children that you did not heal. You will cry over the person to whom you forgot to say, "I love you." You will be measured by one thing, and one thing only, while here on Earth. That is love. So, the next time you are angry, in pain, in resentment, filled with blame and rage, stop and ask yourself, "How does this relate to love?" If you knew that you only had one hour to live and you knew who you would call and what you would say...If you already know, then what are you waiting for?

I find it strange that people who say you need to be saved from the depths of Hell base their judgments on something that most of them have never experienced. Hell was a village outside of Jerusalem where people burned their garbage. It was always burning, smoldering, and was filled with smoke and the stench of garbage. Jesus used the word "Hell" as a metaphor. You are not going to go to Hell when you die, no matter what you do or don't do. You have never, never done anything wrong. The word "sin" means, "to miss the mark." You have merely missed the mark for being here. You have forgotten to hit the purpose of your soul. Instead, you have followed a path that your mind or EGO has humorously created for you. Unfortunately, Christianity attached the Holy Trinity of fear, guilt, and shame to the term sin. Yet, if you are shooting a bow and arrow and you miss the bull's eye, does it make you guilty? No, you have simply missed the mark. This idea of following the path of the EGO versus surrendering to the path of your soul. This is what many Christians would say is the difference between following the devil and following God. Now, you can learn to listen to music of your soul and hit the mark of your mission. But regardless of what you do, you will not fail. It is impossible. It is impossible for you NOT to get to God. Thus, all roads lead to God. Some roads are more directed, effortless, and fun! Other roads are bumpy, but regardless of which road you choose, you will always get to God.

Does this mean that you should do whatever you want without care or concern about possible consequences? NO! Everything that you think, say, and do—as well as the motive behind everything you think say and do—creates karma. There is no right or wrong, just outcomes for everything that you think, say, and do. "As you sow, so shall you reap." If you are filled with fear, anger, blame, and resentment, your life will be Hell on Earth. On the other hand, if you evolve and learn to express unconditional love, you will experience Heaven on Earth. Your mind can choose to tune into the matrix of Hell or the matrix of Heaven. All "Matrixes" are come down to either—a matrix of Love or the matrix of Fear.

3

Seeing God Everywhere

What if God is not some "male" being sitting on his throne in Heaven, casting his judgments upon everything you do while dictating every moment of your life? (As one of the Judeo-Christian names for God is "Elshadi," which translates into "the breasted one." But, if this is true, then this of course would imply that God was/is a female. The Catholic/Christian Church couldn't have that, now can they?) What if God is not a male who is waiting for you to die so that you can plead with him to let you into Heaven? What if God is not a male who will throw mercy on your soul, saving you from eternal damnation? Rather, what if God is a matrix that is woven into all life, everywhere—in ALL things?

To the writers, directors, and producers of the movie, "The Matrix," I cannot thank you enough. Whether it was metaphoric, intentional, unintentional, or by random chance, you have explained the truth about this reality in a remarkable way. A matrix is what perceived reality becomes. Reality is based on your perception of it. Ana Nis writes, "We don't see things as they are, we see them as we are." Because of this, you can tune into whatever reality, or matrix, you wish. The one you tune into is largely based on the decisions, events, and experiences you hold in your "auric" field from the moment of conception to the time of physical death. (The auric field is the electromagnetic field that surrounds the physical body.) However, there are also "imprints" or other matrixes in your auric field that were created in other lifetimes.

Your auric field senses and perceives things before you do. It also acts as a magnet in the sense that your thoughts become an instruction guide for the auric field. Once your auric field is filled with enough like thoughts or imprints, it will create and attract into your life that which reflects those thoughts and imprints back to you. Thus, the idea: "Change your thinking, change your life."

If you have a matrix that surrounds you, and if the matrix of God is woven through all things, then it becomes very natural for us to see God everywhere. The more we think in terms of reality as a matrix, it becomes increasingly impossible for us not to see God. It becomes impossible for us not to see all life as interwoven and interconnected. It becomes impossible for us not to see the ONENESS of all life, everywhere. It becomes impossible for us not to become One with God. As we tune into the matrix of God, we let go of fear and become the matrix of love. We become God. Again, there is only the matrix of love and the matrix of fear. But in order for us to tune into the matrix of God, we must heal our own matrix and imprints of fear. I believe that we as a race make the following decisions about ourselves, which create imprints deep in our own matrix (or auric field). These keep us trapped in the matrix of fear and stuck in the cycle of karma and reincarnation. Often, traumatic events from previous lifetimes lead us to these decisions. (Later in this chapter, I will explain how this relates to previous lifetimes and illness.)

- I am a victim.
- I am not wanted.
- I am unworthy.
- No matter what I do, it won't make a difference anyway.
- I am not understood.
- I am powerless, hopeless, and helpless.
- I am not safe here on Earth.
- I am unable to protect myself.
- If I fully give of myself, I will get hurt or betrayed.
- It is not safe for me to love.
- I cannot trust anyone.
- It is not safe for me to feel.
- It is not safe for me to express my feelings.

- I am not enough.
- I didn't do enough.
- I am not capable.
- I cannot handle it.
- I am being punished.
- I have been left all alone and am lonely.
- I need another to make me complete.
- I am guilty.
- I am unlovable.
- I have been discarded.
- I didn't see it coming. Therefore, I am unable to protect myself.
- I have to depend on others to survive. I cannot depend on myself.
- I am not going to get what it is that I really want. So, why bother making the effort.

Once these decisions have been made, they control our lives until we become clear of them. They are based on a distorted perception of self. When Jesus proclaimed, "I am the light, I am the way, and I am the truth." He was not stating these to be righteous. (As a master is not called master because he himself says so. A master is called master, because those who witness him say, he is master) Rather, they were a proclamation of his identity. They were a testimony to his mastery of his own self-perception. They were his I AM that I AM. Yet, when a child does something that is bad, s/he learns that they are bad. They cannot distinguish between the punishment of the behavior and the punishment of them. This in psychology is called the looking glass self. How do I know that I have done a good job, unless I have been told that what I have done is good? So, if a child's actions are labeled as bad, and a parent fails to point out the difference between bad actions and a bad person, the child learns to perceive itself as being bad. Thus, their self-perception becomes I am bad. Then this perception becomes the identity of the child. This identity becomes their reality. I AM bad. Now, notice the most powerful words of and for God, I AM. Now, attach bad, victim, lacking, unworthy, etc to I AM. Now, you have, a false God. "Thou shall not worship any God before me" "Thou shall not worship false Gods." When your self-perception turns into your self-identity, you create your reality as a false God. Your I am (ness) becomes your state of being, your being (ness) then creates your experience. Jesus was taught from day one, to perceive himself as the messiah. The word messiah or me-si-ah implies to see that God is me. Or in other words, to say YES God is me. As a child of God, can you image what you life would be like right now, if you were taught to perceive yourself as magnificent, brilliant, talented, gifted, or even to be Christ-like? "Behold, I AM the Christ." I am a child of God. I am the light, I am the truth, and I am the way. Your perception of self is vital in what you experience in your life. As you discover to see yourself through the eyes of God, your life will become miraculous. I am God's beloved with whom She is most pleased. See your self as your Angels do and you will perceive yourself as a powerful miracle allowing God to express through you. Allah, literally means, "allow." When you look in the mirror, see your light in your eyes, allow that inner light to expand, love it, and learn to perceive the Christ in yourself. "When you see the Son in the Father you will see the Father in the Son." When you see the Christ in yourself, you will see the Christ in other people. (And vise versa) When you perceive the truth of who you really are, and own it, you will be the light, the truth, and the way. God perceives you as the beloved, the Christ. God truly does believe in you.

Are your wheels spinning in your mind? Once you start thinking in terms of reality as a matrix of self-perception, self-identity, then you can be open to miracles and you will see God in all people-including yourself—and in all things, everywhere.

Now, let's go back to these decisions and perceptions and how they keep us stuck in the matrix of fear. Let's say that as a child you were sexually violated. This violation creates an imprint or matrix that says, "I am unable to protect me. I am guilty. I am bad. I am dirty." This imprint also has a biochemical component to it that remains in the body until it is released. No matter how hard you try to block this event from your memory, the matrix remains. Often, it is the woman who was sexually violated as a teen who gains weight to protect herself from being attractive. Her imprint is, "If I am beautiful, then I will be violated again." Energy never dies, it only transforms.

Therefore, these imprints act like magnets to shape our reality. You must realize that everyone and everything has a matrix around it. If your matrix is imprinted with the thought that "I am not enough," then your world will reflect that. Your auric field will continually draw experiences into your life that reflects, "I am not enough." This is the law of attraction. Because there are plenty of people out there with the matrix that says, "I am better than others," you will attract these people into your life. Then you will measure and compare yourself to them, and in doing so, will get to be right about not being enough. Are you begging to see the implications of accepting life as a reflection of your matrix? Which matrix are you willing to tune into to?

What happens is that we attract people, places, and events that reflect back to us what is occurring in our own matrixes. Do you see how powerful you really are? All of it is a reflection of you. Thus, the world becomes your mirror; you can see all aspects of yourself, both light and dark. Many people want to learn from Jesus, Buddha, Sia Baba, or Mother Mary. Yet, the person who can teach you the most is that no-good SOB that lives across the street. That person would not be in your life if it were not for the patterns or imprints in your matrix. This is karma. This is what you came here to resolve. I hear many people refer to their life as a mess because their Moon is in Cancer. When the stars were set into motion at your birth, you received the astrological imprint that will influence your entire life. It was given to you to transform. Unfortunately, for most of us, instead of transforming our Moon squaring in Pluto, we became stuck in the dark aspect of our astrological configuration. More often than not, our imprints keep us stuck in the past where, according to the law, we will create the same experiences over and over again, lifetime after lifetime.

This concept can also be applied to Vietnam veterans who suffer from post-traumatic war syndrome. Their matrix of reality has become so distorted that they have forgotten how to turn off the matrix and imprints of war. The war experience is stuck in their matrix and remains "on" all of the time. What we don't realize is that this matrix can be switched off. Likewise, we have switched the matrix of God off, but it is still there. It is in all things and in all people. We just need to turn it back on. This is just like a situation in which someone who could walk at one time becomes paralyzed due to an accident. The body remembers how to walk because the matrix of walking is still there and can never be taken away. The matrix of God has always been within you; it never left. So, what if the matrix of walking could simply be turned back on again? I believe that it can.

In his best-selling book, *Ageless Body Timeless Mind,* Deepak Chopra, M.D., tells an incredible story of how memories at the cellular level, if changed, can produce changes within a person's lifestyle. He tells of a woman who was to receive a heart from a younger male. Now, at no time prior to the heart transplant did she eat at McDonald's or drink beer. However, shortly after the heart transplant operation, she began to crave McDonald's food and beer. As it turned out, McDonald's and beer were the young man's favorite food. This implies that a matrix of awareness exists at the cellular level. If new information can be stored in this matrix of awareness, then physiological changes will result.

(Deepak Chopra, M.D., is an endocrinologist and is considered by many to be the pioneer in the field of alternative healing. His numerous best-selling books include *Ageless Body Timeless Mind* and *Quantum Healing.*)

Here is another example of how this works. Let's take a parrot. A parrot does not have a tongue, vocal chords, or physical brain capable of producing speech. Yet, how does it recognize and reproduce speech? What if the parrot has a matrix of awareness or a matrix of consciousness that connects into the matrix of speech? Or what if the parrot's matrix is simply connected to into the matrix of consciousness itself. This is similar to what Carl Jung meant with his idea of the collective unconscious. It is this interaction of the matrixes that enables a parrot to replicate speech without the necessary vocal chords.

Now, let's explore this idea of the matrix of consciousness a bit further. As we become aware of this matrix of God, we can clearly understand how the hundredth monkey phenomenon could happen. In the late 1960s, researchers were studying the behavior of monkeys in the Galapagos Islands. They noticed that when a monkey ate a potato, it was a very messy process because the potato was covered in sand and dirt. One day, one of the monkeys washed the potato off with water before eating it. A domino effect then occurred. Like magic, all of the other monkeys on that island began to wash their potatoes before eating them. Then, monkeys on surrounding islands, who had never seen the first monkey wash a potato, simultaneously began to wash their potatoes. This implies that if enough beings of a race or species do something, then everyone else begins to replicate it. Once one person does something, it is placed into the matrix of consciousness so that anyone can do it. If Jesus can do it, anyone can do it. We are all one.

Now, think about the implications of this. It is simply mind blowing. What if healthy cells could communicate with diseased cells? What if the matrix for walking could simply be turned back on for a paralyzed person? What if the matrix of health could replace the imprint of disease and illness? What if the body could re-create itself? During the past few years, I have demonstrated that breast augmentation through hypnosis works! Lipid cells in the breast can be easily replicated in the body of a woman. I can increase a woman's bust line by two inches in as little as two hours! I have done this live, on the air, with before-and-after measurements taken by another woman! I am convinced that the body is designed to re-create and regenerate itself. Likewise, when you break a bone, the only thing that a cast does is set the bone in place. Your body does the rest—new cells, new connective tissue, and new bone masses. It re-creates itself and you end up with a bone that is no longer broken. Your cells are in constant replication. The following excerpt is taken Dr. Keith D. Clark's book, entitled *You Are Sharp Enough To Be Your Own Surgeon*.

> The physical body that each of us possesses (or possesses us) is roughly 50 trillion cells. About 30 billion of these are nerve cells. Everyday millions of cells throughout our bodies are being replaced. This takes place through the normal process of attrition and replacement. Indeed, 98% of our body is replaced within one year. The remaining cells are replaced the following year. In fact, 10% of all cells in your body are replaced every three weeks, 25% of the cells are replaced every 5-6 weeks. The cells that make up our skin are totally new every 30 days. The cells that make up the soft muscle tissue of our internal organs are replaced in two to three months. The liver is replaced within six weeks, while the stomach lining takes as little as four days. Some cells, such as those closely involved in the process of digestion, are replaced as rapidly as every five minutes! (Clark, p. 5)

You see that the matrix of regeneration and re-creation is always working in your body. You simply need to learn how to use this matrix to create healing. The pattern of perfect health is within your matrix of consciousness. Since your body is designed to re-create and regenerate itself, you just need to turn that matrix back on again. Here is an open letter from a Viet Nam Vet who took the time to discover how to turn the matrix of feeling and mobility back on.

My name is Wayne and this letter is being penned after spending 12 hours—over a period of 2 days—and receiving 12 treatments with Dr. Kelley Elkins I am 53 years old/young and I have been in chronic/severe pain for 34 of those years. Much of my physical pain can be traced back to my tour in Viet Nam, where I was a door gunner in a helicopter squadron.

Like so many others, my chopper was shot down while on a mission. My injuries included a separated skull resulting in severe migraines; blurred vision; and low, dull ringing in my ears. I suffered a dislocated shoulder, knee, and a cracked knee cap, several cracked ribs, a collapsed lung, cracked jaw bone, broken leg, wrist and ankle, a deep bone hip bruise, broken nose, and bruised kidneys, internal bleeding and a sundry of bruises and contusions. I was unconscious for 30 days, received the Last Rites twice, and was basically given very little chance of surviving my many injuries.

However, my physical pain was nothing compared to the mental, emotional, psychological, and spiritual pain/crisis experienced. After my crash, I spent 16 months in various hospitals where doctors tried to piece me back together the best that they could through surgery and physical therapy. Unfortunately, only my physical ailments were addressed. I was labeled anti-social with suicidal tendencies. (Imagine that!) Once they deemed me well enough physically, I received a medical discharge. The physical pain was overwhelming and triggered the abuse of drugs and alcohol to the point of extinction.

Meanwhile my emotional and mental capacities were falling apart at the seams. I experienced flashbacks, deep-rooted shame, rage, fear, guilt, blame, suicidal thoughts, and a need to withdrawal from everyone. Ironically, the more that I tried to numb myself, the more severe the pain; flashbacks, deep-rooted shame, rage, fear, guilt, blame, suicidal thoughts, and alienation intensified. My abuses were nearly killing me.

Thankfully, all of my pain drove me to my knees. I experienced a total break down and then my real war began...Through God's Grace and Love, I finally realized that I dearly wanted to live, not exist, not merely survive in my numb, dumb, and dead "Blackness." With all of my heart and soul, I began the journey back to the light. Many hours, days, weeks, months and years were used up attempting to heal and grow. Many traditional methods were used and explored. After years of struggling, a new crisis arose. I ruptured a disc in my lower back, which required surgery.

Due to the pain, I was given powerful medication and my downward spiral began anew. I fell deeper and deeper into my "Blackness." I went from one traditional treatment to the next, and nothing would relieve the pain. I lost my will to live. I was at a loss as to where to turn next. I finally got to the point where I didn't want to go on any longer; I just wanted to go into oblivion.

That is when I met Dr. Kelley Elkins. While what he was saying seemed, shall I say, strange, his gentleness, depth, and honesty intrigued me. So, I decided to try one last time to find release from my pain and self-imposed exile. On Saturday, March 27, 1999, I went to Kelley in hopes that he could assist me in my healing. Yes, I was eager to try. Yes, I was scared beyond belief. Yes, I had intense doubts and fears. Yet, what else was I to do? So, with high hopes, and deep fears, and much disbelief the treatment began.

The first thing that struck me was Kelley's insistence that he was only a facilitator and that I was the actual healer. All I needed to do was have faith in myself; the process and that I could heal if I chose. This is due to the fact that I am a child of God and that God promises us we can have abundance, wholeness and unconditional love. The second thing that struck me was the gentleness of the procedure. The third thing was his compassion and intuitiveness. Fourth, I experienced a feeling of energy due to the release of pain, followed by a sense of peace.

With each treatment, the pain diminished. It was replaced with warmth that soon spread throughout my entire body. By the end of the second day, I knew that my hopes had not only been met but also surpassed beyond my wildest imagination. I left Kelley a NEW PERSON. Not only was I pain free, there were other wonderful effects as well. The ringing in my ears was gone. The blurring haze has departed. My sense of smell increased. I felt a warmth-vibrating deep within that feels life giving and healing. I feel alive and whole for the first time in many, many years, if not the first time in my life.

I would like to encourage anyone, especially if they are a Vietnam Vet, to make an appointment with Kelley and see what he has to offer. When all else has failed, what do you have to lose except your pain? It was a truly amazing healing experience of the Mind/Body/Soul...In conclusion, I would like to quote, Martin Luther King "Free at last, free at last, Thank you God, free from pain at last." I pray that you open yourself to this experience and that you find release, peace, and LOVE.

Wayne

You may visit Dr. Kelley Elkins at: **http://www.anextstep.org** I encourage you to make an appointment if you need to free yourself from traumatic emotional imprints. I would also like to extend an invitation to Christopher Reeve to make an appointment with Dr. Elkins. The body remembers how to walk. In my opinion, Dr. Elkins has techniques that can turn that memory back on. "Superman," you have nothing to loose and everything to gain.

Here is another example of how these imprints influence our health. Let's say that as a child, your father abandoned you at the age of 5. As a child, you grew up measuring and comparing yourself to children who did have fathers. Thus, you developed a deep resentment around this issue; at an emotional level you were constantly longing for what might have been. This imprint created a pattern within your matrix that said, "People who love me will leave me, so it is not safe for me to love." In order to deal with this, you began to crave sugar. In fact you ate so much sugar that you developed diabetes. Have you noticed that whenever you are lonely and depressed, you begin to crave sugar? Now that you have this imprint of abandonment in your auric field, you will attract relationships that reflect this back to you. Thus, you will continue to consume sugar until you create serious health problems for yourself. Do you understand the cyclical nature of the matrix? Do you understand that emotional imprints are the underlying cause of "dis-ease"? The word "dis-ease," means just that—you are not at ease with yourself. Once you heal the imprint of abandonment, then you heal your resentment. Once you heal your resentment, you will have a new matrix that doesn't feed off of sugar. Again, matrixes feed into each other due to the law of attraction. Since the body re-creates itself, you will be healed of diabetes. This is how it works.

So, how do you turn the matrix of God back on? You must first begin to see the matrix of God in all things, people and events. As you see the matrix of God everywhere, then you will see the matrix of God that is within you, that is you. "When you see the Son in that Father, you will see the Father in the Son." When you see the Christ in other people, you will see the Christ in yourself. As you become aware of the matrix of God that is you, then all things in your life will be healed. If you are in need of a healing and you have been praying for one, STOP waiting for the voice of GOD to speak to you. The matrix of God can be very gentle and soft, but you must be willing to drop expectations as to what it is going to look like, feel like, or sound like. You must surrender to the unlimited ways that the matrix of God can work through you. For example, a friend might say to you, "You know, I just saw the movie, "Blue Turtles," and it was very moving. I think that you should go and see it." Then you go home, turn on your TV, and see an advertisement for "Blue Turtles." Later that evening, your mate comes in and says, "I just ran into Bill and Tina. They could not stop talking about the movie, 'Blue Turtles.'" If you are asking God to answer a question, pay attention to things that come up more than three times. That is God's answer. "The question is not, who does God talk to, but rather, who listens?" Neale Donald Walsch, CWG.

God loves us unconditionally. We are completely forgiven in the eyes of our creator (no matter what we do, period). The truth of the matter is, from God's eyes, you have *never, never* done anything thing wrong. You are completely innocent. However, planet Earth doesn't let you get away with anything. You can try to hide from yourself, but the matrix of God on Earth won't allow it. You might be able to delay it, or put it off for a while, but eventually, the matrix will catch up to you. Have you ever had an argument with someone or left an issue unresolved? So, what do you do? If you are like me, you just avoid it all together, right?

One day, you decide to go to that specialty shop that is a good 60 miles out of town. This is your favorite place and you know that the person you are in conflict with never goes there. You need to get away from the stress and tension of the situation so you head out to the Winds of Spirit Coffee and Gift House. You feel great; your favorite music is playing on the radio. There is no traffic on the interstate and you just can't wait to get a cup of that incredible joe the restaurant serves. Most important, you know that your friend hates coffee, hates the drive, and is at work. There is no way she is going to be there. As you pull into the driveway of the Winds of Spirit Coffee and Gift House, you think you see your friend's car. You shrug it off as a coincidence. Then you walk into the café and there she is...just too completely ruin your perfect day. No, she is not there to ruin your day; this is the matrix of God at work. This perfect matrix is telling you to stop running and deal with this. I know that all of you have experienced this, because this is the reflective quality of the matrix of God. It reflects back to you where you are in the moment. That is why your life is perfect just the way it is. However, we waste a lot of time and energy focusing on how wrong, messed-up, and screwed up our lives are. Then we want to blame the world, the government, our parents, whomever, instead of seeing our life as a reflection of where we are. The good news is that you can change. As you allow your matrix to change, your life will reflect those changes back to you.

Now, do you see the interconnection of the matrix of God? This is how it works. That is why it is possible to experience miracles. "Ask and so shall you receive." We just don't want to listen. We just don't want to see. We just don't want to believe. Your auric field is constantly bringing to you whatever you project into it. Yet, your matrix is filled with too many imprints, including those from previous lifetimes. Let's say that in a previous lifetime you had one true love. You were "soul mates." The love you shared in that time and place radiated out to everyone around you. Your love was so perfect that it made others jealous, to the point that you were killed—literally stabbed in the back by your own brother—because he wanted your wife for himself. That imprint, that trauma, doesn't die. Energy cannot die; it only transforms, remaining in your matrix or auric field until you clear it. Therefore, you will create relationships based on the belief that people cannot be trusted and you will be betrayed. Again, this is your matrix, the reality that you are tuned into. This is what will be reflected back to you. That is why people are born with birth defects. They are carrying imprints of trauma into their matrix from the time of conception. You may have a genetic predisposition toward a heart defect, but it takes the imprint of a traumatic event to trigger the genetic defect, illness or disease.

I am convinced that our auric field, our matrix field, is so busy reacting to stimuli that it literally prevents the body from healing itself. If your auric field is allergic to medication, then the medication won't work. If your matrix is constantly in fear and terror, your body will break down and all of the traditional treatments will fail. On the other hand, if you change your auric field or matrix field so that it doesn't react to a stimulus but is neutral, your body would automatically heal anything. It is designed to re-create itself. The reactions of our fear-based matrixes prevent it from doing so. For those of you who are skeptical about the ideas and concepts of the auric field, you may want to read *Infinite Mind* by Dr. Valerie Hunt, Ph.D. She is probably the most noted expert on the study of the human auric field.

However, it is vital to understand that all of the imprints in the world cannot compare to the matrix of God—the health, healing, prosperity, abundance, and joy that is within you—right here and right now. We just don't want to see it. No, we want a "big bang," a vision, the big voice. But as a matrix filled with consciousness and aware of all things, the matrix of God takes on all forms and is woven within all things. No amount of karma, astrology, or predestination can compare to the power of a joyous soul that filled with a pure heart. When you are ONE with the matrix of God, all things become possible.

I can be an immature, irresponsible, manipulative jerk. Yet if the matrix of God flows in my life, then I promise to you that the matrix of God will flow in yours. When you tune into the matrix of God, it goes out of its way to create miracles in your life if you are willing to allow it to do so. You must be willing to ask for it and then let go of how it is going to happen. "How" is none of your business. That is why miracles are called miracles. If you knew how, then miracles would cease to exist. Here are some stories from my life that enable me to say, "I KNOW that the matrix of God is working in my life today."

Since my near death experience, I have had numerous encounters with angels, divas, and entities that most people would call out of the ordinary. A few months ago, I was in Wal-mart to pick up a few things. I saw a young Hispanic couple with their toddler in the aisle next to me. As I approached the young boy, he developed a huge grin on his face, he looked at me, then his auric field seemed to expand, and he called *me* in perfect English, "Deepak Chopra." Needless to say I was in tears. I thought to myself, *how did this young child possibly know anything about Deepak Chopra, let alone know how to pronounce his name correctly?* Here, the young child allowed God to speak through him. It reminded me of whom I will become. He was also telling me to stay on the path and don't give up.

A couple of years ago, my life was not working. I was in the "dark night of the soul," as they say. One day I woke up and cried out, "God, I want to hear that I am doing something right for once. I want to hear that I am on the right path. Not only do I want to hear that what I am doing is of value, but I want to hear it from a hot looking Hispanic woman. Not only had she better be hot, she had better be stacked. God! I want 'gazongas' God! Do you understand? *Gazongas!*"

About an hour later, I was walking to my psychology of communications class and there was a tap on my shoulder. I turned around and a beautiful Hispanic woman looked at me and smiled. "I just wanted to let you know that I really love your radio show and I am glad you are talking about the book *Conversations with God*. I think that it is great." Yes, God understands what gazongas are.

Also around that time, I was very mad at God. As stated previously, my life was not working. I screamed at God one morning, "I need money! I am broke, God! Money! Cash! NOW! Las Cruces s**ks! God, it f**king s**ks! Here I f**king am in Las Clueless, Las f**king Clueless that is. I am stuck, f**king stuck, right in the middle of the goddamn desert!" (Later in this book I will talk about why I was sent to the city of the crosses.) As I continued to rant and rave about the poverty, the act-nothing-do-nothing, manana land of Las Cruces, New Mexico, I received a phone call from a cocaine addict. He felt that hypnosis could help him out with his 10-year addiction.

The following day, he arrived at my office about an hour late. In fact, I was just about to leave as he pulled into the driveway. I thought to my self, *another f**king no-show*. He came with a friend, and was he was jittery. After about 30 minutes, he relaxed. His friend could not believe what he was seeing. "This is amazing," he whispered to me as I took the addict into a deeper, altered state of consciousness. After about an hour, I brought my client out of a very deep trance. He was in tears. He had not experienced that type of relaxation since his addiction began. He hadn't had a line in a week and was on the edge. He finally realized how relaxed he was.

"On my way up here, all that I could think about was doing another line, but that desire is gone. I feel great! Thanks," he said. He proceeded to pull out a wad, and I mean a wad, of one hundred dollar bills. He looked at me and said, "You've helped me, and now I want to help you. Take whatever you want."

I looked at him and said, "What?"

"Take whatever you want; I don't need this any more."

Then I became caught up in my judgments. I thought to myself, *I really need money, but I can't take it because it is drug money*. So, I accepted only what I charge for a session.

Now, stop and think about this. We must confuse the Heaven out of God. Just the other day, I was screaming at God for money. God gives me money and I say no. We ask for what it is that we want, it is given to us, then we reject it. Again, how it happens is none of your business. So, if you are asking for money and you don't want it to be drug money, make sure that you clarify that, got it?

In 1993, I was a waiter at 82 Queen, a charming, romantic fine-dining restaurant in Charleston, South Carolina. A man from England came into the restaurant, and for five days in a row ended up in my section. On the last day,

I was taking his order and an inner voice said, "Talk to this one about sacred geometry." At the time, I was watching a set of videotapes called, "The Flower of Life," by Drunvalo Melchizedek. These tapes explain the mathematics and origin of life, based on a geometric pattern known as "the flower of life." On that day, we had an hour wait and I was "in the weeds" with six tables. My initial response was, *Yeah, right.* As I walked away, I was pushed back to the front of the table, and again that inner voice said, "Talk to this one about sacred geometry." Reluctantly, I asked him if he was a math teacher.

"Why did you ask me that?" he smiled.

"Well, I am watching these videotapes on sacred geometry right now, which I am sure you have no interest in."

His mouth dropped, "Drunvalo Melchizedek?" As it turned out, he was looking for the same tapes and wanted to know how he could get a set of them. I explained to Rodger that the tapes did not belong to me, but I could put him in touch with the person who gave them to me. We exchanged phone numbers and that night I received a phone call from Rose Mary—the lady who had lent me the tapes. She said that if it was all right with me, she felt it was important that I give Rodger the set of tapes in my possession. I agreed. The following morning, I met Rodger's son and gave him the tapes.

A few months had passed without me hearing anything from Rodger or his family. Then, one day, I left work early as it was extremely hot and business was slow. On my way home, that inner voice returned and said, "Please go directly home, we ask that you do not stop anywhere." At the time, Charleston was new to me and I liked to walk around the historic battery and waterfront. However, I decided to listen and walked directly home. As I opened the door, the phone rang. It was Rodger, calling me from France. He explained that Drunvalo was going to be in Cope Crest, North Carolina, and wanted to know if I would like to go. Without hesitation, I said, "YES!" I wanted to know how much was it going to cost and if I could get tickets.

"Don't worry," he said, "it has all been taken care of. Everything has been paid for. Thank you for the set of tapes. Enjoy."

So, from November 13th through 19th, 1993, I attended an incredible workshop given by Drunvalo Melchizedek. Why? Because I was willing to allow the matrix of God do the work. I just listened, trusted, and took action. There are no accidents or coincidences. As Albert Einstein said, "God doesn't roll dice with the Universe." The universe can and will orchestrate miracles for you if you simply get out of the way. In my opinion, the flower of life and the mer-ka-ba are the matrixes of God within all things. They are "The Force."

In 1995, I needed a place to stay. I still worked at 82 Queen. As I walked into the magnificent courtyard I thought, *God I need a place to stay. I cannot pay a deposit, nor can I sign a lease. I must be compatible with the roommate and I can only pay $350 or less a month.* As I finished that thought, the owner, Joe S., looked at me and said, "I just sat you four tables, get ready." From the moment that I walked into the door until I left, I was busy. I made more than $200 that night. I was so busy that I completely forgot about what I had asked for earlier that evening. When I went home, there was a message on my answering machine. "Mark this is Darianne. I need a roommate—you don't have to pay a deposit, you don't have to sign a lease, there is no long-term commitment. It is $325 a month. Can you move in this weekend?"

In the time between Summer II and Fall Session of 1996, I went to visit a friend in Portland, Oregon. On my way to Oregon from New Mexico, I spent a morning in Sedona, Arizona. Sedona is one of my favorite places in the world to visit and I felt that it was an excellent opportunity to get charged up for the long trip a head of me. I arrived in Sedona about 8:00 am and I went to airport rock where and I had a strange experience of having numerous flashes of energy run through my body. Sedona is a place where many "new age" people gather to experience the reported "vortexes" of energy...(Since 1989, I have been there 10 times) I love it there. Anyway, I felt "altered" and a little light headed so; I went into town and ate some breakfast. After breakfast I went to bell rock and then onto Boynton canyon. The air was clean and the sun was warm. The red rocks of Sedona generated a deep feeling of peace within me. It was about 1:00 in the afternoon and I felt that I had a really incredible time and I wanted to hit the road. I am a "power" driver, when I drive somewhere, it is usually straight through. However, this time something strange happened to me. I cannot explain it. Within an hour of leaving Sedona, I was asleep at the wheel. I was absolutely exhausted. So, I pulled over and got a hotel room. Needless to say, I went directly to bed only to wake up 14 hours later. I woke up feeling like I had slept for 2 days. I felt like I had a lot of time to make up so I was anxious to get on the road and head for Oregon. 12 hours later I was going through the heart of California's wine valley. Soon I started complaining to God about how long this was taking and that it was costing me too much money. I called out, "if you want me to continue, and then give me a sign." Before to long, my gas tank was on empty and I was checking the exit signs for gas stations. Thirty miles later, running on fumes, I pulled into a 76 station. My gas gauge was below empty. I recall that gas was around $1.00 a gallon back then. I put in 2.00 and the gas pump clicked. I felt that this couldn't be right, as it would take at least $15.00 to fill up an empty tank. So, when I went to put more gas into my tank, gas came spewing out of the car. I checked the fuel gage and it was completely full...It was well above the full mark. I guess I had gotten my sign. Upon returning from Oregon, I had to go and take care of my class registration for the upcoming semester.

I went to register for fall classes at New Mexico State University. The lady at the registrar's office quickly informed me that I could not enroll for fall classes since I still owed monies from the previous semester. Now, at no time did she see the list of classes I wanted to take. Even if she did, she couldn't have recorded them since the system automatically places a block on registration documents when accounts are not up to date. I went to the financial aid office, picked up my student loan money, preceded to the accounts receivable office, and paid my tuition bill. After lunch, I returned to the registrar's office to complete my registration. On my way there, I called out in my inner mind, *God if you really want me to complete my degree, give me a sign, because quite frankly God, school s**ks the big one.*

With my registration documents in hand, the lady at the terminal asked me for my student I.D. number. As she entered the number into the computer, something amazing happened. Low and behold, I was registered for all of the classes that were on my registration paper—the ones she had never seen nor entered into the computer. They were listed in the same order as on my paper, at the same times, and with the teachers that I had selected, without a single "class closed" marker. Her mouth dropped and she shook her head in disbelief as she said, "Someone up there is watching over you."

I responded, "Yes, that is becoming more and more apparent to me."

You see, my registration had already been done through me. It was already done. When Jesus raised Lazarus and walked on water, he never said or thought, "Oh s**t, how is this going to happen?" Rather, he KNEW that it was already done through him. Jesus's faith in the matrix of God that is within was so great that it became a KNOWING. Jesus demonstrated his KNOWING. "Be still and KNOW that I Am." Be still and KNOW that I

AM WITHIN YOU. The only thing that we are here to do is to demonstrate our KNOWING.

Unfortunately, we have learned to demonstrate our matrixes of fears, doubts, and disbeliefs. We have forgotten to remember our connection to the matrix of God that is within us. True salvation is about remembering our connection to our souls. As we connect with our inner being, we begin to connect with the matrix of God. As we connect with our soul, we begin to see all life as a reflection of us. Life is our mirror, showing us where we have not yet learned to demonstrate our knowing. Every person you meet will reflect back to you the areas you have not yet mastered. Therefore, all life becomes a matrix, showing you all aspects of yourself, especially those parts that you would rather not look at. Which matrix do you want to tune into? Which matrix are you willing to allow yourself to see?

4

Messages From the Masters

Yes, I have had many visitors in the dream state who speak to me. Jesus, Mother Mary, Thoth, Isis, but most frequently it is John the Baptist. I first heard of John the Baptist from a close friend of mine, Patty Lou Fetters. She played me a recording of the "Out of the Ordinary Show" from KIEV in Los Angeles, California. According to the host, Joe Albiani, Gerry Bowman entered into a trance state and channeled an entity that called himself "John the Baptist." Shortly after listening to a few shows, John the Baptist found his way into my dreams and began relaying many messages, both for humanity and myself. Even though some of these will read as if John is talking to me directly, he is actually speaking to everyone, including you.

Messages from John the Baptist

- A master is not called a master because he himself says so. A master is called a master because those who witness him say that he is master.

- We never use the truth to be right, we never use the truth to score points for our Ego, and we never use the truth to make others wrong.

- The Kingdom of God is within you. Why do you seek anything else?

- If one would live in the moment, what fear would they have? What fear could they have?

- Why do you worry? It does not matter what name you may give it or how you may call it. Rejoice, for the lord is always with you. Rejoice, for the lord made this day. Just realize the lord that we are talking about here is YOU.

- Love is who you are. Be Love.

- Why do you seek that which you already are? (Why seek God? Rather, experience God.)
- Power cannot be given unto a child. However, you must become like a child before you can receive the power that you seek.

This refers to the difference between "childish" and "child-like." "Except ye be converted and become as little children, ye shall not enter the Kingdom of God." Children are fully present in the moment, are playful and spontaneous, and always tell the truth. Most importantly, they use their imagination.

> To see life through the eyes of a child
> Everything is new, everything has meaning
> Questions are asked, answers are yet to behold
> Colors are brighter
> Sight has insight
> And tasting becomes a cosmos
> Colors, Smells, Tastes, Experiences
> And this Overflow
> Is not enough to quench the thirst of Curiosity
> Sensations Perceptions and Emotions
> Without Knowledge
> There is only an Innate Trust
> That the World is a Safe Place
> Life from these Eyes is true Living
> ~ Mark Patterson

- If you want to see God, then look in the mirror.
- If others label you as inadequate, that is their problem, not yours.
- Expansion is that what you fear? Allow your creativity to flow, dear child; allow your creativity to flow.
- See the light in the mirror. As you learn to love that light in the reflection of the mirror, you will come to know that you are a wonderful human being with much to share.

- When you are willing to accept yourself, as you are now, in the moment, you will become very powerful.

- Do you really want to experience your life as anything less than Jesus?

- You view surrendering as a weakness. Surrendering is a great strength. You must be willing to allow yourself to work with both your strengths and weakness. For in love both our strengths and weakness become diluted into one.

- You are the beloved and we rejoice in your presence.

- Love yourself

- There is not a single moment that goes by in your life that you are alone. You are never alone dear child, never. We are always with you.

- Learn to see yourself in all things, all people, and all places. Your life is a direct reflection of you. Here is an example:

Two different people look at the same picture. They both see the same shapes, colors, and textures. One person says the picture is incredible and delights in it. The other person hates it, complaining that it is too simple. These are two different responses to the same picture. But are they really seeing the same picture? Or are they seeing themselves as reflected through that picture, that person that place, that object? Life then becomes your mirror. It will reflect back to you all aspects of yourself. Learn to see what is being reflected back to you. Use life to show you to yourself, for we are all ONE.

- If you were wise enough to know, what question would you ask? (The answer, of course, is contained within the question. If you were wise enough to KNOW, you wouldn't ask the question in the first place.)

- You already know the answers to the questions that you ask. Validation? Is that what you seek? Validation? Trust, dear child, trust and know that who you are and what you do is important and of tremendous value.

- Service to mankind is always first.

- Stop being a martyr to your own joy. It is simply not necessary unless you choose it. If you choose it, then so be it, but it is not necessary.

- There is nothing that you cannot change. You may not know how or why you created it, but once you accept that you chose it, and then you can change it. There is NOTHING that you cannot change (unless you become victimized by it). Be not the victim, be the creator.

- Why do you allow others to determine your worthiness? You are worthy simply because you are.

- Allow your feelings of inadequacy to be what they are, for they can move you and guide you into a place of power.

- Why do you bring the past into the present? Now is all there is. Does the past really matter right here, right now? NO, then DROP it!

- We want you to look in the mirror and say, "I LOVE YOU."

- Why do you fear love?

- Why do you measure and compare yourself to others? Do you think that God does?

- If one is in their head with another, then you are really not with the other individual.

- The plan is there is NO PLAN. There is ONLY NOW.

- The end of the world is at hand, but which world are we speaking of? Physical mental, or emotional? (I believe that the mental world—duality consciousness—is about to come to an end)

- Life is a gift. You are a gift to the world. Your gift to the world is your gift to God.

- Guilt and shame are like a ruse, a facade that hides the light from you. What is there that you cannot love within yourself?

- When you see the light in other people, you will see the light in yourself.

- "When you see the Son in the Father, you will see the Father in the Son."

- You may think that you can start completely over by moving to a new location. Just realize that you take yourself wherever you go. (Wherever you go, there you are.)

- Enlightenment looks just like this. It looks just like this room, or this wall. Enlightenment is not something that you over-achieve into. It is something that you allow. Relax into it. Do you think that you are going to create "super flatulence?"

- Throw away the cape. (Stop trying to save everyone. Save yourself first.)

- Meditation is how you focus your attention. As you learn to focus your energy towards one goal, your life will become very productive. You tend to divert your energy into too many different things. This is not a race. There is nowhere to go. You will always be here.

- You have learned to listen to your inner voice, now listen to your heart.

Messages from Jesus

- Tell them to take me off the cross. I can no longer carry their pain. It was never my job to do so in the first place. (The crucifixion is a metaphor that was used by many cultures prior to Christianity. It symbolizes the burdens one carries for others. What are you placing on your heart that does not belong? Jesus carried the burden of showing that death was an illusion, as he did not die on the cross but resurrected.)

- Why do you not believe in the miracle of the NOW? Why do you not believe in the miracle that is you? Why do you not open your heart to the divine that is within? Within your heart is where you will find me.

As a child, I used to dream that I was inside my bedroom closet, which contained all the gifts and toys I could ever possibly want. Anytime that I felt lonely, unwanted or rejected, I found myself inside that magical closet. Anything that I wanted was there waiting for me. It has taken me 25 years to realize the story behind that dream. Everything that I, or you, could ever want is contained within the closet of your own heart. "Above all things first ye seek the Kingdom of God." Yes, that magical place is within all of us, right here, right now.

- You are LOVED.

- When you listen to your heart, you will find God.

- Be still.

- Yes, it is true that I said, "I am the way and I am the truth." But that did not mean that you could not do it without me. For you are also the light, the way, and the truth. I just left a pattern that was to be followed.

Do you understand this? Please allow me to rephrase it. You can get to God just as you are, right now. You don't have to believe that Jesus is your savior, nor do you need to believe in Buddha, Krishna, Sai Baba, or any Baba. However, if you can't believe that you can do it by yourself, then you can do it through Jesus. Unfortunately, the church forgot to mention that you could do it by yourself. They focused on the part that said that you had to do it through him. (Actually, it seems that the church forgot to mention a lot of what Jesus taught) John 10:34: "Is it not written in your laws, I say ye are Gods." Again, the church became caught up in the messenger, not his message.)

- There are only opportunities to learn forgiveness. (Forgiveness is not about looking the other way. It is about, foregoing the pain that the other person or event has inflicted upon you)

- Why do you not believe? Faith in your self is the key!

- I am with you.

- There is only love and fear. Fear is the absence of love.

- I am not the answer, love is.

Messages from my Angels

These are messages from my angels. For the most part they are talking to me. However, many of these messages will apply to you.

- Listen to the music of your own being.

- Trust the inner voices of your own being.

- It gives us great pleasure to hear your thanks, as your thanks is music to our ears.

- Going within on a daily basis will be of great benefit.

- Foods that are of nature are more fueling for the body.
- Meat and dairy products will cloud your visionary body.
- How we long to hold you; how we long for you to KNOW that we are holding you.
- You take yourself way too seriously.
- Play more.
- Sex is important to us and there are quiet a few of us feminine angels who would love to have sex with you. So, stop pretending that women find you unattractive. As long as you believe that women find you unattractive, you can be safe and not experience love. Surround yourself with women. There is nothing guilty or shameful about sex. We envy your ability to achieve orgasm. Sex is a great gift. However, we caution you that it is not to be misused. (I was 20 and very shy when they told me this.)
- We are you.
- You cannot comprehend how beautiful you are from our perspective. We do not see your body; we see your soul. That is indeed a sight to behold.
- There are many beings about you. The divas and fairies play around your hands. They will always bring you good luck.
- You came here with many memories of the future. It as if you know what is about to happen just before it does.
- Acting "overly special" is the misuse of energy and it will return itself upon you.
- You are not alone.
- Act as if you are in awe of life. Make every moment sacred.
- Stop punishing yourself.
- Trust your inner guidance; as you have a tendency to dismiss it.
- You are like a child who wants to play at the amusement park all day, but one of these days you will need to grow up.

Messages from Mother Mary

- We want you to know that you are loved UNCONDITIONALLY.
- Dear child, know that you are loved.
- You are blessed. You have many gifts. Use them, for they are needed.
- Trust that you have it within to create whatever it is you are wanting.
- Trust the process of life. Even when it appears that you cannot, trust.
- We are joyous in your presence.
- You cannot fathom the love that we have for you.
- You are protected. You are safe. You are wanted.

A message from Thoth

Thoth was an Egyptian God. According to Drunvalo Melchizedek, Thoth provided all of the information that is taught in the Flower of Life workshops.

- You humans forget how important you are to us. You send us information, just as we send you information. We (the ascended masters) could not complete our work without you.

A message from Kryon

Kryon is an entity channeled by Lee Carroll. Kryon came to me in a dream one night after I listened to one of Lee's tapes. I perceived Kryon as electromagnetic waves shaped like a tube torus (i.e., a doughnut). Kryon literally blasted a wave of energy into my etheric body, which contained a very simple message:

- Feel the love that your inner being has for you. Always focus on it and you will do great things. Kryon then left.

I woke up glowing, feeling wonderful. I think that most people have found that their lives have been more chaotic during the past few years.

Americans seem to be losing it emotionally. Have you noticed that time has shifted into warp speed, that there don't seem to be enough hours in the day to get everything done? I look into people's faces and see exhaustion and burnout. While Wall Street continues to expand and thrive, nearly 40 million people live in poverty in the U.S. I am going to paraphrase something Kryon said in a recent article that finally made sense. I have seen this in many people.

> Before most of you came here, your inner being knew that between 1996-1999 this time frame would be the "end of times," as you would call it. Within, you created an imprint of self-termination that was to be activated during these times. Yet all of you have now shifted this need to self terminate, but the imprint is still there. Because you have shifted this need to self-terminate, you have also activated within you a new strand of DNA. Now you are dealing with a new DNA that is instructing you to go forward while the imprint of self-termination is fading away. You literally have within your body an energy that it was never designed to carry.

I think that this explains a lot. If you think that this idea of self-termination is crazy, here is another quote from Tara Sutphen who is channeling her spirit guide, Abenda:

> There is a will within many to destroy what they have, because with survival comes a sense of belonging to the earth and all that it means. Rather than focusing upon survival, it is time to live in your world. Open your mind, your eyes and your senses to what all life can be. It is your divine right. Accept your right and you will know the path of life.

Again, that is why we must address the "dark" that is within us. In truth, love is the answer. As you learn to love all aspects of yourself, you will integrate your own darkness. The plan of light within you will prevail.

A message from Abraham

Ester and Jerry Hicks channel Abraham. I was walking to class one day when Abraham came to me and said: "Do you really think that you are more intelligent than God? Trust life Mark, trust the process. All is well in your life and you are guided. Trust."

Indeed, I am guided and these are just a few of the messages that I have received from our nonphysical friends. I wish I could trust their guidance more, and ultimately trust my own heart and soul. There seems to be a fine line between our guides guiding us, and our guides steering us off the path as a test, to see if we will listen to them or trust ourselves. I am reminded of a conversation that I had with my friend, Sherry, the other day. We happened to receive the same information on this very subject.

Your guides will change their advice as your awareness changes. Here is an example. For the past year, I have been focusing on going to Naropa University for my Master of Arts degree in Transpersonal Psychology. Transpersonal psychology excites me; I am passionate about it. Transpersonal psychology looks at a person from a holistic perspective—body, mind and soul. It gets to the cause of a problem rather than just treating the symptoms. My guides have been pushing me to go to Naropa. Unfortunately, a degree in transpersonal psychology is not taken seriously in our society; I would probably be laughed at. Then, my awareness shifted. I thought, *Why not get a masters degree in Industrial and Organizational Psychology? I could apply transpersonal and spiritual concepts in corporate settings where they are the most needed. The people who are into transpersonal psychology are going to see me. The people who are not will avoid me like the plague. With this degree, I could reach more people and become a trainer in-group dynamics.*

Wouldn't it be great to have a spiritual environment at companies such as Microsoft, Dell, Intel, IBM, GM, and Ford? Wouldn't be wonderful if the corporate world placed a sanctuary in every building? Wouldn't it be great if corporate decisions were made through a relationship with a "higher power"? Now, this gets me excited. I have a stronger sense of purpose now. I have something to focus on. This also gets my angels excited; they guide me as I follow this plan. I will continue to study transpersonal psychology on the side and incorporate it into my work. As you shift your awareness, your guidance follows that shift. And so it is.

5

How do you start over when you feel have nothing to start from?

On June 26th 1996, I left for Las Cruces, New Mexico, after being guided by "spirit" to move to the land of the crosses. I was informed in my dreams that I would go to the desert and meet my exotic looking Hispanic soul mate and create a life of my dreams. I was really reluctant to follow this advice since I had spent the past few months in Iowa trying to convince the state of Iowa and the University of Iowa to allow me to do some archaeological digging in the Coralville reservoir. As, I was guided by spirit to return to Iowa from Charleston, SC, to find some relics that were supposed to have been placed there thousands of years ago. Spirit promised me that this was going to be the greatest discovery in the history of humankind. After nearly two months of various negotiations with state officials and people at the University of Iowa. After hearing numerous promises by spirit of fame and fortune the chase for the ancient relics came to a crashing close. I was soon told over the phone, "sorry, we don't know who you are, and we no longer wish to talk too you."

In the summer of 1993, the state of Iowa experienced unprecedented flooding. At the time I lived in Charleston, SC. However, in October of that year I had an opportunity to go back to Iowa to witness the aftermath of the flooding of that summer. One particular area of note was the Devonian fossil gorge in Coralville, Iowa, which was unearthed as a result of the extensive flooding. As I walked into the fossil gorge the reality of the flooding had set in. I was amazed at what had been unearthed. The limestone and the granite with fossil's that existed in the Devonian era were incredible. However, I immediately noticed something very peculiar about the fossil gorge. In the exact center of the fossil gorge stood a soft dirt mound in the shape of a brain.

I looked around and felt that there was simply no physical way that mound should have still remained. It should have been complete dissolved along with the other dirt and soil that had been unearthed in the flooding. There was a large stone in the shape of a triangle that had someone been placed directly in front of this mound. Thus, it managed to divert the water around it. Even with the mysterious triangle in place, the pressure exerted by the flooding going over the mound would have been enough erode it completely away. According to certain principles in physics that is. But what was most peculiar about the mound was the composition of its soil. As I looked at the embodiment of the banks around the fossil gorge the soil was much lighter in color than the color of the dirt mound. I knew that there was something really strange about this mound. As I approached the strange mound, I could feel a pulse. It had a pulse to it that was connected to what I could see in my inner mind as crystals. In my third eye I could see that about 10 feet below were these green colored crystals that had an incredible light too them. They had this strange pulse to them. It was if they were keeping some kind of time. Or that they were orchestrating time itself. My mind was brought back to the rest of the gorge when my Mom called over to me. I knew that there was something that needed to be further explored. I returned to Charleston, SC, with a lot of questions in my mind about this mound. I decided to call a friend who was gifted with automatic handwriting and I explained to her about my experiences at the mound. I asked her if she would channel some information about the experience and what was at the center of the mound in the Devonian fossil gorge. When she channeled her writing came through that there were in fact two crystals placed there and that they were to be activated at a later time. After exchanging numerous phone calls, ideas, and upon my completion of an Associates degree, that later time had arrived.

In the summer of 1996, I went to Iowa to work with my automatic handwriting friend to convince local authorities to allow us to excavate the area of the fossil gorge. It was an emotional roller coaster up one moment down the next from day one. Every day we were receiving new information from our spiritual guides about what we were to do next. She was receiving information via automatic handwriting and I was receiving information in my dreams. Time and time again our information was identical, therefore we believed it too be valid. In our pursuits we found for every person who was curious and supportive we had three whom though that we were absolutely crazy. There was one man whom I will call, "Mr. Blue" who stated and I quote, and "If there is anything there and it needs to be protected, well, leaving it deep in the Earth is exactly where it should belong." There was a huge concern that if we could bring these artifacts, scrolls, or crystals, to the surface, they would have to be placed in the geological vault for rare findings. Mr. Blue had no interest in going through the paper work, which was required to get the alleged artifacts into the vault. I recall at the time, I just wanted to give up and go back to Charleston, SC. I even think that our guides informed us that, "our services were no longer required." However, a couple of days later I experienced something remarkable in my dreams. Many of previous incarnations came to me and they began to speak too me. At first I felt that I was being "psychically" attacked. Then they convinced me that they were there for my benefit. Soon they all began to merge into one. Then they merged into my body as if they were making peace with each other and myself. My lifetimes had integrated into one. I woke up feeling so peaceful. It was incredible. I had also received the message that our project was still unfolding. On that afternoon, we received a phone call from the dept of Geology at the University of Iowa. We became very excited when they reluctantly admitted that the composition of the soil in the mysterious mound was not of this Earth. Intuitively I felt that the soil would match to lunar soil. So, we began to talk to various people in Flagstaff, Arizona, at the Center for Non-Earthly materials. Some how, we got them to match a lunar soil sample with a sample from the mound in Iowa. They were over 97% identical. That is when I called the University of Iowa Geology department to inform them that we had clear evidence that we should be allowed to move forward with our project. Then I was very abruptly informed, "we don't know who you are, and we have never spoken to you, and we no nothing about this." Click. I guess we got too close for their comfort zone. Boy, I was pissed off. I felt that I had given up everything in my life, for this purpose. I felt that I had given everything to God and I trusted whole-heartedly for absolutely nothing, squat, zilch, zip, nada, and a wild goose chase. My friend however, she didn't give up anything. She was still working and would go back to work soon. But me, I felt that I had been dealt an empty hand. So, at the moment I didn't really give a f***k about what my guides had to say about the whole thing or my life any more until, the next day that is. We were instructed to go down to the mound at sunrise and we would be allowed to "ascend" into Heaven and experience something really incredible. Reluctantly, my friend and I agreed. So, at 4:30 AM we headed down for the Coralville mound.

Shortly before 5:00 AM I witnessed this world completely disappear. I had literally left this world with my body and walked right into another one. There was this incredible feeling of love. I felt that I was one with God. I could not believe what was taking place. I really had experienced ascension. Not only did I experience ascension but my friend did as well. This time there was a witness. We were promised that "God" itself would raise the crystals and the scrolls and that we were to take them to the press. Unfortunately, when we "came back" there was no container, no crystals, or no scrolls. There was no fame or fortune. It was just an incredible experience of ascension. Did my friend and I really walk into Heaven with our bodies? YES, it was undeniable. That afternoon I walked in my close friends Chiropractic office he took one look at me and said, "Wow, you are glowing." He was right. I could not believe that I accomplished something that most people feel is a lofty goal. People spend lifetimes trying to learn how to ascend, but I was given the incredible gift from spirit at the age of 26. But my ego could only focus on the lost fame and fortune. In my anger and haste I was getting ready to return to Charleston, SC, when I decided to ask my automatic handwriting friend a question. "What should I do next?" Her handwriting said, "You should go to Las Cruces, New Mexico." Then I asked my friend who is a Chiropractor to "muscle test" my body for what was the best thing for me to do at the time. Well, my body was split between Charleston, SC, and Las Cruces, NM. Charleston, SC, was better for my financial situation, social life, and having fun. Las Cruces, NM, however, was better for spiritual growth, emotional growth, and there were people whom I was to meet. At the same time my friend in Portland, Oregon called me and said, "You need to go to Las Cruces, there is a Hispanic female there who is your soul mate. You and here will have lots of babies and create a beautiful home together." (This is a side note. In all honesty, I took my near death experience and I swept it under the rug so to speak. Then when I was 25 a woman in Portland gave me a phone call in the middle of the night. She came across my phone number in a very unusual set of circumstances. She proceeded to describe the events of 2/1/86 and went onto describe events from my childhood. Keep in mind that we had never met or spoken with each other prior to this phone call. Needless to say, it was a real wake up call for me to get on with my life and to become a messenger for God.) So, at the time I had good reason to trust her advice to go to Las Cruces, New Mexico. It also was the same thing that my dreams had told me just a couple of weeks prior. Another close friend of mine in Iowa City,

Iowa had just accepted a position at New Mexico State University in Las Cruces and he was after me to complete my four-year degree at NMSU. So, all guideposts were pointing to the desert Southwest. I chose spiritual and emotional growth over financial stability and fun. Thus, I went forward and headed to the city of the crosses and moved to Las Cruces, New Mexico.

When I pulled into New Mexico State University, I literally had $27.00 and some change in my pocket. I called my friend whom I was to suppose to stay with until I could move on campus for the summer session, but the only thing that I could get was his answering machine. So, I was stuck between a rock and a hard place. I decided that I needed to make some phone calls to find out what my next step was going to be? So, I went over to a pay phone and spoke with a local Flower of Life facilitator whom I discovered over the Internet a couple of weeks prior. He gave me directions to his center for natural healing. Upon walking in he introduced himself and then he handed me a paper that he felt that I would be interested in. It was an article from a man named Alton. Alton was a gentleman from Australia who taught an advanced version of the Mer-ka-ba meditation. It was called the Melchizedek method. The article was faxed to his office just a few days prior read, "On June 21st, 1996, at 4:44 AM two crystals were activated and placed in the magnetic grid of the Earth…" The letter continued by stating, "the other two crystals would be activated at a later time." I could not believe what I was reading. This was the exact time and the exact date of my experience just a few days ago. I even recalled a dream where I was in space and I placed four crystals in a gird above the Earth and we were told after our ascension experience that we had activated two crystals. This though was too strange. I remember the goosebumps that I got upon reading that letter. How did a man in Australia know anything about events that took place in Coralville, Iowa? It was just too weird. Thankfully, my new friend found a place for me to stay. (My friend in Oregon also confirmed that this was exactly what had taken place, without me even telling her about my experience) Anyway, four days later my financial aid came through and my student housing opened up at NMSU and I was ready for my journey into the desert Southwest.

I began to explore the campus of NMSU. I found myself outside the Corbett Center where I saw a sign posted for DJ wanted. I guess I have always wanted to be a radio personality. I always wanted to have a radio talk show, similar to the one Art Bell had. So, I went in and spoke with the programming director and asked her if I could create a morning talk show that related to the paranormal? She wanted to know more. I told her that I wanted to have psychics and astrologers on the air. I wanted students to be able to come into the booth and get live readings over the air. I knew that it would be a big hit with the college students. I asked her if we could do a trial show. I felt that I could find a couple of psychics to come on air within a week or so and that it would be loads of fun. She said that she would be willing to give it a try. So, with that we agreed that the show would air on Monday at 10 AM in a couple of weeks. I went into the local new age bookstore and began to grab business cards of local readers. I found a couple of readers who were very excited and could not believe that a local radio station was willing to place this type of programming on air. I placed flyers around campus and I made phone calls to various people. This program was generating a lot of excitement. On the day of the show, we had students lined up at the booth. Once on air, we had non-stop phone calls. We had an instant hit. I had a numerologist and an aura reader. It was incredible. Soon it was the talk of the new age community. People were calling me to be on the show and students wanted to know when the next show was going to air. Within a couple of months I was generating a lot of attention. I found myself being interviewed by radio, TV, and newspaper. Then by December I began to promote my first workshop, "Past Life Regression and Future Progression." I was allowed to speak about myself and my workshop at the Mastery in Life Center in downtown Las Cruces. The MILC was sponsoring me for this presentation. Well, my first workshop brought in over $2000.00 and I had 75 people in attendance. This was absolutely unheard of. Big names like Gregg Braden and Ken Page would come to Las Cruces and only get 10-15 people. I got 75. I absolutely felt, that I was creating the life that I wanted to live. Yet, just six month prior I had only had $27.00 to my name. Just six months prior I had nothing, I barely knew anyone, and I my place to stay was up in the air. But I discovered my passion, radio, and things began to happen. I created everything even though it felt like I had nothing.

And so, we come full circle to the title of this chapter. How do you start over when you *feel* that you have nothing to start from? The truth of the matter is, you never have had anything. In fact you have always have had everything. "The Kingdom of Heaven is within you." I mean what more could you need? Why do we seek *anything* else? In fact the only way to create anything is to create from nothing. All creation takes place from the void. Where do your thoughts come from? Where does the energy come from that produces the thought? "In the beginning there was darkness, and God said, let there be light." The ability to produce a thought from nothing defies most principles of physics. Yet, all creation, all creativity comes from the void. You are designed by nature to transform nothingness into "somethingness." You are here to transform the non-physical into the physical. This is perhaps God's greatest gift. There is nowhere, where you can transform the void into the physical. You can only do the miracle of creation while you are in a body. Do you understand now what a remarkable gift your body is? "Be you perfect, for the kingdom of God is within you." You are whole complete and you lack absolutely nothing. You are nature's greatest miracle. You are a creation of God, from the void, from the darkness of a womb into a child of pure potential. This is creation itself. So, what we feel is nothing, is actually everything. When it appears that we have nothing we are given the opportunity to use our creativity. There is not a greater place to be then in our pure potential of the void. The only thing that God created was your soul. Your soul has an absolute knowing of its ability to transform the void into your dreams. It knows that it is perfect. It is everything. It knows that you are an incredible gift from God. Most importantly it knows that God believes in you.

6

God Believes in Me

A popular TV show on Angels recently stated, "Fear of God leads to wisdom." As I heard this, my heart sank, and I knew that this was the problem with our religions. How can you fully trust something, which you are taught to fear? How can you develop a relationship to a God whom we are to be afraid of? How can we experience oneness or the at-one-ment with God when we believe that we are to be in fear of it and its judgment against us? I continued to think about this quote, and I saw that this fear of God is exactly why we believe that God is separate from us. In fearing God, we remain in the illusion that God exists outside of ourselves. Then I thought how could I get people to believe in a God who believes in them? How do you convey to some one who has AIDS, cancer, who has been betrayed, left homeless, who was raped, exploited, or sexually violated as a child? Or to anyone who lost a child by a drunk driver, who lost a loved one, who has been taken advantage of, whose heart has been broken, that not only that there is a God, but a God believes in them? Then, I thought, about the question, "Why does God allow bad things to happen to good people?" "Why does God allow bad things to happen, period?" Well, I am not so convinced that God does. Rather, I think that it is our soul that creates circumstances, which enable us to evolve. Again, the only thing that God created was our soul. Events in our lives that are "painful" are merely opportunities to learn forgiveness. Or as a close friend of mind would say, "Another f**king growth experience." In creating our soul God gave us all of the tools to change anything, be anything, or do anything. All power comes from within our soul. Before incarnating here, you agreed to do one thing and one thing only, evolve. You agreed to rise above your fear-based emotions and express unconditional love. Unfortunately, it is our mind that convinces us that we are victims. It is our mind that keeps us stuck in our fears. Thus, Jesus said, "You cannot serve two masters." You see your mind or EGO wants you to serve it, not your soul. Your EGO wants to be "right" that you are unwanted, unworthy, and unlovable. Your EGO wants to be "right" that you have been betrayed. Your EGO wants you to believe that what others have is better than what you have. Your EGO wants you to believe that you are incapable of achieving great success. In a sense your EGO becomes "Satan" or the principle of opposition that resides within you. Your soul then becomes "Christ" or the principle of truth that also resides within you. With this in mind, the Bible then becomes a metaphor for the journey that the soul takes while it is on Earth. The written battles of good vs. evil in the Bible are symbolic of the battles that take place between your mind and soul. Thus, "sin," means missing the mark of your soul or missing the mark of your "purpose." When you follow the path of your EGO you are in "sin." Yet, when you are on the path of your soul, then you are following "God's" Will or what I like to call, "Divine Will." At any given moment, in your heart and soul, you always know what to do. Your mind however, convinces you otherwise. Your mind prevents you from surrendering to the purpose of the soul; it keeps you from trusting your heart. (This is the principle of opposition, or "Satan" at work)

However, there is not a single more important relationship in your life, than the relationship that you can develop with your inner being, your soul. As you embrace your inner being, you will discover your own perfection. You will re-member that you are whole, complete, and that you lack nothing. You will see how *YOU* have conspired the events of your life, to show you where you have yet learned self-mastery. You will understand what Jesus meant when he said, "The Kingdom of Heaven is within you." Most importantly, you will *feel* the love that your inner being has for you. You will know that your inner being believes in you, adores you, and is longing for you to acknowledge it. It is longing for you to listen too it. It is wanting for you to be guided by it. It is wanting you to trust it, and surrender too it. It wants you to drink of its spirit. "Drink from these waters and you shall thirst no more." Who you are is greater than AIDS, cancer, poverty, illness, and disease. Doesn't the bible say, "You have been given the armor of God?" As you create an inner intimacy with yourself, you will also discover a God that believes in you. For God knows that within you, you have incredible gifts that are there for you to draw upon. You have all of the tools, to create a life that is based on the laws of grace. For your soul or inner being knows only love. Your mind however, keeps you trapped in the laws of karma and reincarnation. Your mind keeps you in fear, doubt, and it keeps you in slavery to drama. We are addicted to drama. If you don't believe that we are divided within, just look at the last presidential election. "As above so below, as within so without." Is this not an incredible reflection of the state of our minds as a whole? Oh, how your soul is longing, begging for you to develop a relationship with it. For whatever your mind/body field has created, your soul can change. So, how do I come to know a God, who believes in me? How do I develop a relationship with my inner being, my soul? Well, that is the million-dollar question, and sure as Heaven, I have a few suggestions on how to do just that!

If the mind is the problem, then one must learn how to integrate it into the soul. One must allow the mind to surrender to the soul. This does not mean that you are to "squelch" the mind or EGO, as some eastern religions would suggest. Rather, it is the ability to discern the difference between the games of the mind, and the path of the soul. For the EGO is a master just as your soul is, but it is also a "trickster." Your soul will never trick you, for it only expresses the truth. To integrate the mind into the soul one must be willing to acknowledge that they have a soul or an inner being. One must make a decision to discover who they are from the inside out. One must be willing to go within. One must then realize when Jesus said; "Above all things, first seek the Kingdom of Heaven" he was speaking of the huge importance of going inward. In fact, there is nothing more important, than creating a relationship with you. As the saying goes, "I shall go within, or I will go *without*." It is a journey that enables you to discover the God that is within you, and it empowers you to become the Christ that you are. This is the true meaning of Jihad. Jihad is not a holy war of Christianity versus Islam. There can be nothing that is holy about war. Holy implies to be whole and war implies to be in conflict or divided. You cannot be whole if you are in conflict. The original meaning of Jihad implies, "the utmost inner war." It is about getting serious in confronting your inner demons. It is the most sacred of paths. It is only for the most disciplined. It is about going within and declaring a "whole war" on your fears, doubts, and insecurities. It is about confronting your emotional baggage and discovering your God self. Is this not Armageddon? Can there be no greater conflict than our internal ones? So, I wholeheartedly encourage you to declare Jihad. I encourage you to declare a whole war on your fears and fear-based emotions. I fully encourage you to discover your God self. In my opinion, there is not a more effective way to create this inner discovery then through sound, toning, or chanting. The word enchantment implies to become one with God through chanting.

In January of 1994, I attended a talk at a Unity out side of Asheville, NC. One of the keynote speakers was author, Barbara Marciniack. I felt her book; <u>Bringers of the Dawn</u> was simply awesome. I loved every word. I just could not put it down. She channels a group of beings that call themselves the Pleadians. I was very curious about toning and the power of sound. During the question and answer session I asked the Pleadians about toning. They replied, "We are going to give you an incredible gift." They began by stating, "It is our intention that with this sound, we crate a greater experience of unity in this room." Then they made this sound "wooooooo." Then they asked everyone to join them in the toning exercise. Upon 10-15 minutes of this group toning the Pleadians rang a tingshaw bell. They said, and I'll never forget this "is there any doubt in anyone's mind that we are not all one?" The 100 people in that room were in complete unity consciousness. It was an incredible experience. Then the Pleadians continued to explain the power of sound. "It is the start of all creation, in the beginning was the word, understand this?" They encouraged the group and me to be willing to work with toning and sound. So, when I returned to Charleston, SC, I began to experiment with toning. I found that I could create overtones, and hit notes that created a resonance that was simply uncanny. Over the years I have played with toning off and on. However, it has been brought to my attention that this is truly my gift in life. Lately I have been able to hold notes for a minute and a half without taking a breath. The resonance that these tones produce is from the angelic realms. It is something that connects me into the divine. It is as if it is channeled. I have toned for large groups and after about 30 minutes I will look up to discover that most of the people are literally "out" of it. Just like when a stage hypnotist commands a subject "sleep" and they go under. The tones that I channel seem to penetrate with precision the emotional imprints that are in the auric field. The penetrating resonance and harmonics literally cuts the chords of those unresolved issues. I am continually amazed at how it affects others and how it beings me closer to God to my soul.

It is said that to be happy one must forget about themselves. In all honesty I would just as soon do my toning in private and not have anyone hear me. Then when I do give myself permission to tone in front of people I am blown away by what happens. I cannot believe what they say about this gift. I am amazed by the sounds that come through me. It has such a deep impact on people that it would be a great disservice to humanity not to share it. You are given gifts. Your gift to God is your willingness to share them with others.

Happiness is created when you are willing to forget yourself and focus on how your gifts impact other people. This is service to humanity. This is surrendering to your soul's purpose. Currently, I am working on a CD called, *Angels Caressing You, Harmonic Resonance for World Unity*. We hope that it will be available in the spring of 2002. It is a musical massage that caresses and energizes your energy field. It has prayers; toning, chanting, and crystal bowls set to beautiful new age music. We are very excited about it. We know that it will empower people everywhere.

Edgar Cayce predicted that the future of healing would be sound. This past month, I saw a very interesting presentation on healing and sound by Sherry Edwards. She claimed that she could "hear" the notes of the energy field of the human aura. According to Sherry every person is literally missing one note of the music scale in the energy field of the body. Each of the seven chakras or energy centers of the body correlated to one of the seven musical notes. A, B, C, D, E, F, G. She discovered that when you got a person to listen to their missing note, after a period of time, the body would heal itself. Sometimes the healing was instant, in other cases it took over a span of time. Yet, time and time again, the body responded to its missing note by healing itself. One of the most remarkable healings took place on a 14-year-old boy. His kneecap was completely damaged by a farming accident. Sherry simply made him a tape of his missing note and within months he began to re-generate his kneecap. This is documented on video and it is complete with before and after x-rays. My curiosity got the best of me. So I asked my friend if he could check to see which note was missing from my own energy field. My friend, who can muscle test the body from a distance used reflexolgy to determine that I was missing the note of G in my energy filed. The note G correlates with the throat chakra. It is believed that the throat chakra is the last one too fully open in a person's spiritual development. It is the one that connects us into the spiritual realms. So, I called a person who had a set of complete singing bowls if she would record the not G for me. When I got the tape and listened to it, my body literally discovered a new drug. It was and still is amazing. It has brought a deep sense of balance and peace that I have never experienced before. It is remarkable what happens when you get your missing note back.

I believe that Edgar Cayce is correct. The future of healing is sound and that future is now. Sound is my gift and we know how it affects people. We are very excited about this CD and know that it has the potential to impact people in a similar fashion that Sherry Edwards work has. We all know that sound influences consciousness. There are numerous scientific studies on how sound influences behavior. Now, we hope that we can show that sound has a much greater effect than we thought is possible. Here is just an idea on how we think that sound could be used as a healing modality. We know that all viruses are crystalline in structure. What if you could change the frequency of a virus by changing its vibration through sound? Could, cancer, bacteria, and viruses be altered via sound? Destroyed? Altered to the point without causing harmful side effects to the body? The implications are indeed far reaching. The future of healing is sound. It is an incredible gift; I only pray that I find the courage and humility to share it with the world.

You see you have a gift. It is something that you and you alone are truly gifted at. As you discover your gift, and share it with the world, you cannot help but discover a God who believes in you. What if you had cancer and you overcame your cancer? What if your miraculous healing of cancer inspired you to tell others how you overcame this disease? What if you story went onto change one person's life? What if it changed 1000's of lives? God believes in your ability to transform the quality of your life. Regardless of where it is at in any given moment. Is this not your nature, to transform the non-physical into the physical? If you do not believe that one person can influence the world, look at Jesus, Erin Brockovich, Gahndi, MLK, JFK, and many others. You see God created your soul, perfectly. How could God not believe in its own creation? Do you not believe in your own children? Do you not believe in their ability to learn how to walk on their own? Do you not believe in your own child in their ability to learn how to speak? In their ability to ask questions? In their ability to wonder? Do you not believe in your own child? You would not be here, if God did not believe in the miracle that is you.

7
Life Scripting

So, I want you to use your imagination and think about a process that is called, "Life Scripting." I want you to imagine that you are at a graduation ceremony. You have just graduated from the "University of Self-mastery." You are presenting yourself the certificate of graduation and now your are explaining to your fellow graduates, how you obtained self-mastery. This is an exciting process, because it does the following:

1. It gets you to have something to focus on…focusing or learning how to "command" energy towards a goal.

2. It gets you in tune with your "purpose."

3. It gets you passionate about who you are and what you are become.

4. When having the "end" in mind first, your own dialogue will naturally generate solutions to your current "challenges."

5. You are developing a relationship with your inner self. In doing this, you will discover a God, that not only believes in you, but a God who has truly created a magnificent being, with so much to share!

In a sense, you are telling a story about your life, and how you overcame these challenges to create the life that you want to live. In doing so, you are creating the "feeling" that you already have it. You are creating the KNOWING that these events have happened because you are telling a story that explains it as if you have already lived it. You will then realize that you had it all along. For an example, my life scripting ceremony would go something like this:

We have gathered here today to honor the graduates of the "University of Self-Mastery." Our first distinguished graduated is Mark Clinton Patterson. Mark is one of the most inspirational speakers and one of the most influential people of the 21st century. He changed the world and its relationship to God because he believed in a God who believed in himself. His relationship to a God who believed in him, led Mark to write some of the most powerful, transformational, best-selling books that have now been translated into 21 different languages, and read by millions upon millions of truth seekers from all over the world. Noble Prize-winning author Mark Patterson is said to be "The Man who changed our Relationship to God and to each other." It all started when Mark submitted his book "You Are God" to iUniverse.com. From there he allowed his creativity to flow in his next book, "God Believes in Me" a major publishing company knew instantly that it had a best-selling title on it's hands and they immediately said YES to his manuscript. He wrote, "Spiritual Partners," with Betty Ann Jiron. Spiritual Partners created new paradigms for intimacy in relationships for people who came together on purpose while living separate lives. While writing "God Believes in Me," and "Spiritual Partners," Mark Patterson explored his gifts of toning and chanting. This practice of chanting the Garvandana and toning led him to communication with the Angelic Realms and his soul. This inner dialogue empowered Mark to receive the gift of channeling Jon the Beloved and Merlin. As Mark allowed himself to feel the love and adoration that his inner being has for him, he created an incredible life. Soon, he was one of the most sought after spiritual leaders in the world today. As he allowed him self to trust and expand, his world expanded rapidly, beyond his wildest imagination. Within a matter of months, Mark Patterson went from high indebtedness and virtual bankruptcy, to traveling all over the world as a missionary and visionary. His Mystic Life Ministry went to every corner of the globe. His message: "God is within, and as we embrace the God that is within and come to know of the love that it has for us. We will manifest Heaven on Earth." Mark Patterson found himself working with Dr. Deepak Chopra, Neale Donald Walsch, Dick and Tara Sutphen, Lee Carol, Jan Tobler, Gregg Braden, Tom Kenyon, Doreen Virtue, Marianne Williamson, Ken Page, Sai Baba, The Dalai Lama, Drunvalo Melchizedek, and others. For nearly two years Mark traveled abroad promoting his books "A Mystic's Way," "You Are God" and "Spiritual Partners" with Betty Ann Jiron. His Grammy award winning presentation, "Building the Bridge between Religion and Science" was watched by over 60 million people worldwide. It was the most watched TV event in recorded history. Mark Patterson went onto to make a movie with Oliver Stone, called, "The Church." The Church based on his book of the same title was adapted into a screenplay. It looked into the history of the Church and the events that led to the division between the Catholic and Christian Churches. It exposed the harsh reality of the atrocities committed against humanity in the name of God. In an incredible display of technology and astrology The Church created a mirage of images of various people and their incarnation cycle throughout many lifetimes. The Church won seven academy awards including Best Picture, Best Director, and Best Screen play." Now matter, where life took Mark, and no matter how many times he stood in front to large groups of people, he was always safe. It was as if he had an inner voice that directed him, every step of the way. He was always guided and protected in everything that he did. His work with sound, healing, and consciousness won Mark Patterson the Noble Peace Prize. Mark Patterson became an Ambassador to the United Nations, a leader of Goodwill and Peace. He worked with the leaders of various countries to end the pain and suffering of women and children in third world countries. The practice of clitoris mutilations and acid burning of women were put to an end. He became a major spokesperson for alternative treatments for HIV/AIDS. As a UN Ambassador, he helped bring awareness to abusive child labor practices in third world countries.

However, all of his accomplishments would not have been possible, if he did not take the time to heal his relationship with his father, his mother, and most importantly himself. As he healed his relationship with his father, financial abundance began to pour into Mark's life. His practice, stage shows, and job created a steady income of 6,000.00—7,000.00 a month. While he was out working, various people for past life regressions contacted him. He was also able to generate extra income by performing stage shows. As he healed his relationship with his mother, his insecurities became a distant memory. He let go of his obsession that it was always his sole job to satisfy and please women. His relationship with women became healed because he was able to trust that he to satisfy and please himself first, so that he could be in a position to truly give to another. As he healed his relationship with himself, he went out and discovered real happiness! He moved to southern California where the energy of the ocean and the environment enabled Mark to create the life that he dreamed of living. He got involved in softball, flag football, and little league baseball as a coach. It was around this time, when his soul just opened up and he got the word that a major publishing company said yes! He discovered a God who believes in him. He became secure in himself. He was able to pay back various people whom he owed money too. He was able to clear up all of his "bad" debts. His new inner security was reflected by his outer security. Mark decided to take ownership of his life, and he learned how to command energy. He grew up, let go of his need to be dependent of other people, and became a Man. A Man who transformed, uplifted, and inspired, mass consciousness. Mark Clinton Patterson, he is a man who became a leader of leaders, a transformer, who awakened, "Christ-Consciousness" within, and led countless others to follow an inner path to God. He allowed himself to become the vehicle, a messenger of the Divine, Holy, and Sacred. He was born on October 21, 1969, in Des Moines, Iowa. He was a latchkey kid, from a broken home. A single mother who at times received state assistance raised Mark. From meek beginnings, to a "mover and a shaker, a policy maker." Ladies and Gentlemen, with great honor, respect, and admiration, Mark Patterson Cuma-Suma-Luma honored graduate of the University for Self-mastery! Wow! That was fun to write that out! What an exciting discovery! To come to know what it is that you are truly wanting in life. To have your own destiny in mind!

Once you have decided what it is that you want to accomplish life, you can create a life script with the end first in mind. As you are writing your script, you will begin to feel an excitement about the unlimited potential that you have. As you being to feel excited about who you are and what you are to become, you will live your life with *passion*. I am not talking about sexual passion, or lust. I am talking about being passionate about your life. Living your life with a zest and flare for life itself. Passion creates self-actualization. Once you are into your passion, you will come to know your inner self. When you begin to create a relationship your inner self, you will discover a God who gave you all of the tools, to overcome hardship, adversity, to for go pain, illness, and suffering. You will make decisions that come from accepting yourself as the sole authority in your life. You will no longer make decisions that are based in fear, anger, lack, revenge, or desperation. You will make decisions that are based on love, and who you are. You will experience empowerment. You will discover a God who listens to you, understands you, and most importantly, you will know a God who believes in you. You will live only what you love doing; eat only what you love eating, live only where you love living, etc. You will see Heaven on Earth, because the truth is, it has always been "here." Now, you will **experience** it!

8

Religion's Dark Side

All life is a reflection of where we have let learned to demonstrate self-mastery. We have been "programmed" to react out of fear, lack, anger, etc., versus responding only love. Again, the only thing that God created was your soul; the rest becomes opportunities to learn forgiveness. Yes, the universe is very generous with their opportunities to learn forgiveness. Forgiveness however, is not letting someone off the hook. It is the willingness to forego the pain that it has caused you. Thus, true "salvation" is when we re-member our own connection to our soul.

The only difference between you or I and Jesus, is that he re-membered his inner connection to his soul. Thus the atonement: at-one-ment. He KNEW that he was ONE with the God that is within. In his KNOWING he demonstrated the laws of Grace. You and I (us) have continually demonstrated the laws of karma and reincarnation. Again, when Jesus created miracles he KNEW that it was already done through him. He prayed with a pure heart. He demonstrated his KNOWING. The only thing that you and I are here to do is to demonstrate your KNOWING. But we have unconsciously demonstrated our fears, doubts, lack, etc."Be still and KNOW that I AM. Be still and KNOW that I AM WITHIN YOU.... John 10:34 "Is it not written in your laws, I say yea are Gods." As for being perfect: Jesus said, "Be you PERFECT for the Kingdom of Heaven is Within You." Notice the word PERFECT and that comes directly from the man himself Jesus.

Christianity is based on the idea that one must accept Jesus as their savior so that when they physically die they experience Heaven in the after life, correct? Or at least this is what TV Evangelism is selling today. But Jesus' promise to us was that the Kingdom of Heaven is Within Us. It is within us, TODAY, Right Here and Right NOW! So, what are we waiting for? So, my question for you is where is God? More than likely you will say, "God is at the Gates of Heaven" And I will say, you are right. If Heaven is within us, as

Jesus said, then God must be within as well. If God is within us, then we must all be an aspect of God, thus the quote from John 10:34.

Religions create fear, hatred, separation and division of each other. They are the basis of most wars. "We have God, you don't, this is the right way to God, we are saved, and no we are chosen." Claim the various religions. Yet, the very idea of people who are saved, or who are Chosen is based in JUDGEMENT. Yet, Jesus said, "Judge NO ONE for you do not know how they stand in the eyes of God." Yet, this idea of people who are saved, chosen, and "superior" is why we had slavery, Stalin, Hitler, and conflict in the world today. How can it possibly be right? JC said, "Even when you hurt the least of your brethren, you are hurting me." We are all ONE. Jesus was sent here to show people how to end the cycle of karma and reincarnation. This is done through, compassion forgiveness, and non-judgment. Yet, most Christians, and bless your heart, are filled with judgments.

Do you believe that God is love? If so, I want you to stop and think about all of the synonyms that are related to the word Love. Did you notice that Judgment is not one of them? Love cannot judge. It is impossible for Love to Judge and that is why JC said,

"Judge NOT that ye be judged. For the judgment that you have shall be the judgment that you get, and the measure that you give is the measure you shall receive." Unfortunately, Christianity became caught up in the messenger, not his message. "Love God and Love your Brother" If we are God(s) like he said, then the real truth is "Love yourself, so that you may love your brother"

The TV evangelists, the fundamentalists, born-again, the Catholic Church, and most Christians have the masses convinced that their way is the only one way to discover God—their God, that is. They want you to believe that Jesus died on the cross for your sins and that you will die and burn in Hell unless you claim him as your personal savior. They get you to think that you can do whatever you want to in this life and then just before you die, proclaim him as your savior so that you can go to Heaven. There are some crucial errors in this thinking. This is a bunch of buffalo chips and the Church knows it. (Didn't Pope John Paul II admit that Hell was a state of mind last year? Didn't he admit that the inquisitions were wrong? Didn't he ask for forgiveness for the misdeeds of the church? Didn't he ask that the leaders from the twelve churches of Abraham do the same thing?) Did they? No! So, here is a little reminder for them.

1. Jesus did NOT die on the cross. He RESURRECTED.

2. The Bible is NOT God's word. It is the word of inspired men, subject to endless interpretation. Most of the original ARAMAIC bible has been long forgotten and never revealed.

3. Man is NOT a sinner, nor is he born in sin. John 10:34: "Is it not written in your laws, I say, yea are GODS." Jesus also said, "Be you PERFECT..." We are GODS, and the Church has suppressed this truth to control the masses through the Holy Trinity of FEAR/GUILT/SHAME. How can we be "guilty" just fore being here, just for having a body? Sin means to miss the mark. It does not mean or imply guilt.

4. The Second Coming CANNOT HAPPEN because HE NEVER LEFT!

5. The Kingdom of Heaven is within us, it is us, and therefore WE DO NOT NEED TO DIE IN ORDER TO EXPERIENCE IT!

6. What Jesus taught and what the Christian/Catholic Church says he taught and what they teach you are two different things.

Now, let's look at some historical facts!

First, Jesus, or Yoshua, was an ESSENE. Mary and Joseph were ESSENES. The Essene's were a sect group who believed in reincarnation. Because of this, Jesus would have taught about karma and reincarnation.

Second, the many of the first followers of Jesus—also taught about karma and reincarnation.

Third, the original symbol for Jesus was NOT the crucifixion, but rather, a dolphin. (I will explain why this is important later in this chapter.)

Fourth, 2,000 years ago in the Middle East, the term for a young woman was "VIRGO." This was changed or translated to mean "VIRGIN." Mary was a VIRGO, NOT A VIRGIN. Even if Mary was a virgin, back then, term virgin did not mean, not having sexual intercourse, it meant not being tied down to any man. It was also usually reserved for temple prostitutes whose job was to initiate young boys into manhood.

Also, there were NO Caucasians in the Middle East 2,000 years ago. Thus, Jesus would have had a dark or olive complexion. So, this whole idea that the white race is superior because God's only son was white is a bunch of garbage.

The people who knew Jesus knew nothing about humans living in other areas of the planet. Even though there were people in Africa, North and South America and elsewhere, they did not exist in the minds of those who witnessed the times and life of Jesus, including the crucifixion. Therefore, when it is said, "He died on the cross for man's sins," it could have only applied to contemporaries of Jesus.

You must realize that most of us have been taught HISTORY (His-story) from a white, European perspective. To this day, we still teach our children that Christopher Columbus discovered America. Yet, this is a blatant lie. Can you imagine what it would be like if history was taught from a Native American perspective? We might be taught that Christopher Columbus invaded or ruined America. Indeed, we are so egocentric.

Fifth, karma and reincarnation were removed from the teachings of Christianity and the Catholic Church in 553 A.D. at the Second Council of Constantinople by the Nicene decree. This conflict arose between Roman Emperor Justine and Origen's doctrine of reincarnation. "Anyone who believes in the pre-existing soul shall be left in anathema." (Or exiled from the church.) The Catholic Church declared Origen's doctrine of reincarnation to be heresy, as well as the Thirteenth Gospel, written directly by Jesus. Even though, more than 80 percent of all religions teach about karma and reincarnation.

Much of the New Testament was written almost 250 years after his death. I find it strange when a TV evangelist quotes from the Old Testament. I mean wasn't this the purpose of Jesus's life? Wasn't it to liberate people from the old laws? Isn't the Old Testament about karma and the New Testament about grace?

Another thing that I can never figure out is that the TV preacher tells you that 2000 years ago upon the cross, Jesus went into the depths of Hell and he **abolished** sin. Notice the word in bold, abolished. If sin was abolished, it can no longer exist. Then the preacher man turns around and tells you that you are a sinner, born in sin. Either Jesus **abolished** sin 2000 years ago and it no longer exists, or it is still here. If it was abolished then it becomes absolutely impossible for you to be a sinner. Yes, this in only one of many contradictions that the TV preacher will try to get you to swallow hook, line, and sinker.

Finally, the Bible was not translated into Modern English until 1738 AD. All of you know what happens when you tell a story to someone, and that story gets passed onto the next person, and the next…by the time it reaches the 10th person, the original story is distorted at best. Now, if 10 people can't get the original story straight, what do you think would happen to a story that was passed down for more than 1,700 years?

I mean, historically speaking, the "Church" has committed the most heinous atrocities against the human race. The "Church" nearly eliminated an entire race of beings—the Native Americans—on not ONE, but TWO, continents. This was also true in the "dark ages," when the church destroyed the Egyptian mystery schools and the teachings of the Egyptian God, Hathor. Later on, the Church killed off the Pagans and Celtics, and continued its persecution with the Salem witch-hunts. We have been taught that St. Patrick's Day is about St. Patrick, who killed all the snakes in Ireland. There are no snakes in Ireland, only Pagans who were labeled as snakes. This behavior continued into WW II, with Hitler labeling the Jews as "snakes." He killed six million human beings because of this type of thinking. More recently we have seen this "ethnic cleansing" in the former Yugoslavia. It is complete insanity. When is it going to end?

Who made the Church judge and jury of this planet we call Earth? Who? I would also like to know by what law? What right do you have to decide that others are "evil" and then kill them? Yet, you kill in the name of GOD? "My God is right and yours is wrong. Think as we do or die in Hell? We are saved and chosen; you are not." These are people who claim to be saved? People who claim to be chosen—how arrogant are you, really? The people of the Jewish faith say that they are the chosen ones. Christians say that no, they are the saved ones. While the Catholics pray to Mary in hopes of reaching Heaven. The Islamic fundamentalists say that The Koran is the book of God and that Allah is God.

Can you imagine for a moment that you are an Angel? As this Angel, you are filled with grace, vibrancy, intelligence, and love for humanity. From this perspective you can see the past, present, and future. You look to Ireland and you see the Catholics and Protestants killing each other over the need to be right on how to worship God. You look to the conflicts in the Middle East and you see innocent children being killed because people have a great need to be right on how to worship God. Then you look at the Catholic and Christian church, and the number of people, whom were killed during the inquisitions, because they were judged to be unworthy of God's life. You look at the discovery of the "New World" and you look at the Native People who held a sacred relationship with Mother Earth and Father Sky. You see how they were killed because of a religion that deemed them as "savage." You see how religion used fear to convert people or kill those who opposed. You see that the need to be right on how to worship God keeps people in fear of each other. It keeps them divided, separated, and in fear of each other. You carry a deep sense of sadness within the depths of your being. You look to the right and you see God and how God longs for her children to discover the only place where She dwells is within their own hearts. For God knows that if her children would all discover this, then Heaven would prevail on Earth. Then you glance over to the left, you see "Satan." He has a big grin on his face. For he knows that as long as there are people who believe that they are "saved" and "chosen" there will be those who will be viewed as "unclean." As long as this type of conflict between people exists, Heaven cannot prevail on Earth. Thus, "Satan" will always win.

Considering that all of these people are saved and chosen, we sure have a lot of conflicts in the world today. Look at the Catholics and Protestants. Look at the Middle East. Look at what just happened in the former Yugoslavia. Look at 9/11. It is this type of thinking that causes all wars and conflicts in the world. I ask, how can it possibly be right? Religions keep people divided, not united. We are all ONE. "Even when you hurt the least of your brethren, you hurt me." WE ARE ALL ONE. I had a NEAR DEATH EXPERIENCE 15 years ago. In Heaven there is NO religion, there is ONLY GOD.

The greatest crime ever committed against the human race was to tell man that he was a sinner and unworthy to receive God's love. The amount of irreversible damage, separation, hatred, and division that this has caused cannot possibly be measured.

To teach people that we are sinners born in sin, to deny the truth that we are Gods, and to suppress the truth that the Kingdom of Heaven is within us right here and right now, is BLASPHEMOUS. "Judge NOT that yea be judged, for the judgment that you have is the judgment you shall receive, and the measure you give shall be the measure you shall get. GOD IS LOVE. LOVE CANNOT JUDGE, PERIOD. As the above quote states, we are not judged. However, we sow and we reap. This is KARMA. "Judge NO ONE, for you do not know how they stand in the eyes of GOD." In telling someone that they need to be saved—is this not a judgment? Well, what are you doing?

Jesus was a master of his own thoughts. His faith in himself was so great and he was so tuned into the matrix of GOD, that when he raised Lazarus he never said, "How am I going to do this?" Rather he KNEW that it was already done through him. He demonstrated his KNOWING. All of the tests in life occur in areas where you have not yet learned to demonstrate your KNOWING, lifetime after lifetime after lifetime. Jesus was a savior, not because he died on the cross, but because he showed us how to end the cycle of karma and reincarnation. This is done through compassion, forgiveness, non-judgment, and unconditional love. (Yes, I am repeating myself here, but it is so important that you get this.)

Yet, the Christian/Catholic Church is all about JUDGMENT, JUDGMENT AND MORE JUDGMENT. It is caught up in the messenger, not his message. "Love God and love your brother." If we are Gods like HE said, then the real truth is, "LOVE YOURSELF SO THAT YOU MAY IN TURN LOVE YOUR BROTHER."

"God loved us so much that he sent his only Son…" What does this have to do with love? Would you send your only child to a distant planet, knowing that he would be killed by the time he was 33? This has nothing to do with love, NOTHING! It is the biggest guilt trip ever placed on the consciousness of the human race. So, if you are trying to save someone out of love, STOP. It is NOT LOVE. It is a judgment based in fear and control, and it feeds on people's feelings of guilt and shame.

Rather, teach people that we are all ONE, that the Kingdom of Heaven is within us right here, right now, and that we are God's. This, and only this, will end all wars, hatred, separation, and conflict. GET OUT OF RELIGION AND GET INTO GOD. That GOD is YOU. True salvation is about remembering your connection to your own soul, the Kingdom of Heaven that is within you right here, right now. Follow your soul, listen to your heart, and to thine own self be true. This is about following the matrix of the inner Christ, the matrix that Jesus left for us. Since we are all ONE, if one can do it, all can do it.

Jesus left a matrix for us to follow a pattern that would enable us to become like him. "Even greater miracles then these, yea shall do as well." This is why many "new thought" or "new age" churches (i.e., Science of Mind or Unity) refer to Jesus as the "Way Shower" rather than a savior. In my opinion, this is far more accurate.

This is just a side note that I think you will find interesting: The Dogons are a remote tribe of people from the west coast of Africa who have an oral history that goes back 50,000 years. During the past five years, numerous physicists and astronomers have visited the Dogons because of their accurate information on various star systems. Although by our standards they should not know about such things, they specifically know about two star systems Sirius A and Sirius B.

Everything that the Dogons have said has been scientifically confirmed. They obviously did a better job of storytelling than the Catholic Church, because the story was kept within the tribe and did not cross language and cultural barriers. So, what does this have to do with Jesus? According to the Dogons, Jesus came from the Planet Sirius and was a dolphin. This explains why the original symbol for Jesus was a dolphin. The story of the fish and loaves of bread did not come about until 400 years after his death.

Why is it that we know nothing of Jesus' life after the resurrection? Wouldn't that be the most IMPORTANT? But that, too, was suppressed, because it is the only way that the Christian/Catholic Church could say that he "died on the Cross..." Now, back to this Jesus as a dolphin concept. I believe that if Jesus came to you and you were ill, you would be cured instantly. Does anyone know what happens when people who are ill with multiple sclerosis, cancer, or most other illnesses swim with dolphins? They are instantly cured. Kinda makes you wonder, doesn't it?

9

Where was God on 9/11?

I am writing this chapter not to offend anyone. Rather, I am writing these chapters to bring comfort to those who like me have asked why? To bring comfort to those like me who have felt so lonely, powerless, and anxious. To bring comfort to those like me who have had to re-evaluate everything that was once important to them. To let readers know that their loved ones and fellow Americans did not die in vain.

On September 11, 2001, my roommate knocked on my bedroom door to inform me that America had been attacked and to turn on the TV. So, I quickly turned on the television and watched in shock as I witnessed the second plane run into the World Trade Center building live as it happened. I was getting ready to go to work for a meeting. When I got to work, the meeting was set aside and my co-workers and I was glued to the TV set. This was unheard of. How could something like this happen in the United States of America? Yes, I admit that I am somewhat of a conspiracy theorist. And yes, there are conspiracies out there about the events of 9/11 and some of them make very valid points. Others well, not so valid. I personally think that the current war in Afghanistan has more to do with the huge reserve of oil that was discovered off the Capisan Sea, about 30 years ago, than the Taliban and the al-Queda network. I admit though, that it would be hard to find anyone who did not feel that the Taliban should be removed from power. Defacing the shrine of the Buddha was probably the straw that broke the camels back so to speak.

But, if God doesn't roll dice with the Universe, then there can be no mistakes. There can be no accidents or coincidence. For whatever reason, and even to this date, I specifically do not know as to why, but I spoke to CNN correspondent Barbara Olson. (Wife of Bush attorney Theodore Olson) In my dream I tried to talk her out of flying on that airplane. (This took place during my dreams and it the dream occurred just the night before 9/11) I don't know why my soul spoke to her; I just know that at some level of consciousness I did make contact with her. I do not know her, or her family. Yet, I know of many whom spoke to all of these individuals in the dream state. I know many others who have experienced the same thing in regards to the events of 9/11. Perhaps this is why the number of people who took aboard these flights was unusually low.

So, why did September 11, 2001, happen? Were these events orchestrated at a higher level for a purpose? If so, then what possibly could that purpose be? The following message has been passed around the internet and I am including it in this chapter. Then I will make my own comments about 9/11.

> How many of us have heard that question "Where was your GOD when the World Trade Center and the Pentagon was attacked?" Well, I know where my GOD was the morning of September 11, 2001, and she was very busy!
>
> She was trying to discourage anyone from taking these flights. Those four flights together held over 1000 passengers and there were only 266 aboard.
>
> She was on 4 commercial flights giving terrified passengers the ability to stay calm. Not one of the family members who were called by a loved one on one of the highjacked planes said that passengers were screaming in the background. On one of the flights she was giving strength to passengers to try to overtake the highjackers.
>
> She was busy trying to create obstacles for employees at the World Trade Center. After all, only around 20,000 were at the towers when the first jet hit. Since the buildings held over 50,000 workers, this was a Miracle in itself. How many of the people who were employed at the World Trade Center told the media that they were late for work or they had traffic delays.
>
> She was holding up two 110-story buildings so that 2/3 of the workers could get out. I was so amazed that the top of the towers didn't topple when the jets impacted. And when they did fall, they fell inward. GOD didn't allow them to topple over, as many more lives would have been lost.
>
> And when the buildings went down, my GOD picked up almost 6,000, of Her children and carried them home with Her. Reassuring Her frightened children that the worst was over and the best was yet to come.

She sat down and cried that 19 of her children could have so much hate in their hearts. That they didn't choose Her, but another god that doesn't exist, and now they are lost forever.

She sent Her children that are best trained for this disaster and had them save the few that were still alive, but unable to help themselves. And then sent many others to help in anyway they were needed.

She still isn't finished though, She held the love ones that were left behind in Her arms. She comforts them daily. Her other children are given the strength to reach out to them and help them in any way they can.

And I believe she will continue to help us in what is to come. She will give the people in charge of this great nation the strength and the wisdom to do the right thing. She would never leave us in our time of need.

So when anyone asks, "Where was your GOD-GODDESS on September 11," you can say "everywhere"! And yes, although this is without a doubt the worst thing I have seen in my life, I see God-Goddess' miracles in every bit of it.

I keep praying for those who don't believe in GOD-GODDESS, every chance I have. I can't imagine going through such a difficult time and not believing in GOD-GODDESS. Life would be hopeless.

Today is November 21, 2001, and CNN just announced that the actual death toll from WTC I and II was 3,937 people. The estimated cost of the greatest terrorist attack that the world has ever seen is 200 billion dollars. I would like to share with you some numbers that CNN usually does not report. In the gulf war or operation, Desert Storm, 250,000, human beings from Iraq died. 50,000, babies die from starvation each year in Iraq alone. 16,000, women each year in Afghanistan die in giving birth. Close to 30 million people in Africa are infected with AIDS, the entire continent is on the verge of extinction. In the week following 9/11 the stock market lost one trillion dollars. (As of today the stock market average is close to 9900 points. This is above where it was at on 9/10/01 so; it has made up its losses.) Our one trillion dollar lose is greater than the GPA of Iran, Iraq, Pakistan, and Afghanistan **combined**. Microsoft founder Bill Gates is worth an estimated 54 billion dollars. The entire country of Afghanistan is worth an estimated 1 billion. (I am sure that will go up once the oil line is in place) Clitoris mutilations on women are still a common practice in the Middle East. Women in

Afghanistan under Taliban law are forced to wear a complete covering of their faces. Many women are raped and then jailed because the same men who violate them accuse them of prostitution. Many other countries in the Middle East follow similar practices. Under Taliban law a male child who is four years old has more rights than a 21-year-old woman in Afghanistan. Many of us have watched the news and have witnessed the atrocities that women in Afghanistan and the Middle East have faced for years. If it were not for 9/11 would you be aware of the treatment of women in Afghanistan? Or in the Middle East? Would you have been made aware of the poverty, malnutrition, and suffering that these people experience day in and day out? Would you have been aware at all? Would you have simply remained in denial of what takes place in Afghanistan in the postmodern world? I am not sure but I would guess that one of God/Goddess missions in life is to make us aware. It is sad that we as a race are so dense at times; that it literally takes what it takes to get our attention. 9/11? Don't you find it ironic? Isn't 9/11 or 9/11 what we dial in an emergency? Isn't 9/11 a cry for help? Do you think that it is possible God/Goddess orchestrated these events to cry out to us, to say, "You can't suppress women any longer?" "You can't go about your lives acting as if there is nothing wrong in the world today?" "You can no longer live your lives without purpose." I mean if God/Goddess created a flood to create a better race then wouldn't God/Goddess use other forms of destruction to enable us to evolve? How many more Susan Smith's have to drop their children into a lake before we stop violating children? How many more Nicole Brown Simpson's have to die before we address the problem of domestic violence? How many more teenagers will have to shoot each other in schools before we get out of denial that violence in the media doesn't desensitize our children to it? How many more 9/11's have to happen? How much louder do you want God to shout at us?

Didn't 9/11 bring you closer to your family? Did it not open the opportunity for you to heal old relationships that were once closed? Didn't it make you look to God for the first time? Did it not require you to reevaluate *everything*? Isn't it about time? Did it not give you the opportunity to say, "I love you" to those whom most needed to hear it from **you**? Did it not give you the opportunity to learn about another religion called Islam? Did it not give you unprecedented opportunities to learn about the conditions of the world? When the IRA disarmed themselves did you not shed a tear of joy, in hope for world peace? Was that not a miracle in and of it self? Did you not learn about what is truly most important too you? Can you only praise God for the events of 9/11? Can you find that silver lining in the cloud of 9/11? Did it not make it realize that you and your brother are ONE? Did it not bring religions in America closer together? Did it not bring humanity closer together? Thank you God/Goddess! The following are messages that I have posted on my web site at **http://www.angelfire.com/nm/mesmer**, which are related to 9/11.

Jihad? Holy War? I find the term Holy War rather strange. As, I observe war and I find nothing holy about it. I find this a really confusing term as they imply two different things. Holy implies to be whole while war implies to be in conflict or divided. One cannot be whole if they are in conflict? So, why is there so much emphasis on Jihad or Holy War these days?

Or have extreme facets of Islam lost the true meaning of Jihad? Just as most extreme fundamentalist in Christianity seem to have lost the real meaning what Jesus really taught? The term Jihad implies "the utmost inner battle." Jihad is about confronting your inner demons not the external ones. It is the most sacred of tasks. It is our willingness to discover who we really are. It is about getting down to business and facing your self. Thus you are declaring a "whole war" on your fears, doubts, and worries. You are devoting your phase of life to discovering the God/Christ/Allah/Buddha that is within you.

Now, isn't this Armageddon? Can there not be a greater conflict a greater war than the one that is within? Satan originally meant "the principle of opposition" that is within you. This is the mental aspect of your self who tells you that you are unworthy, bad, and not good enough, etc. While the Christ represents the "principle of truth" that is also within you. The principle of truth represents the all of the LOVE of who you really are, the Christ/God/Goddess self. This is why JC said, "You cannot serve two masters" Because the principle of opposition wants you to serve it, not the principle of truth. Unfortunately, yes, they are both "masters" So, is this Jihad? You had better believe it. It is about time.

I encourage you to fully participate in Jihad and declare a "whole war" against your doubts, fears, and insecurities and re-member the light of the world that you truly are.

Currently, there is a top-secret covert operation that you are being asked to be a joint force in. It is called Operation F.O.G. FOCUS ON GOD. It is so secret and covert that it only takes place within the confines of the inner most places of your being. Operation F.O.G. requires patience, strength, compassion, non-judgment, and most importantly unconditional love. Your ability to achieve success in this strategic campaign called Operation F.O.G. requires a new level of thinking. It will require you to seek spiritual solutions to mental, emotional, and physical challenges.

Yes, your ability to succeed in F.O.G. will be tested. It will be tested in ways never be seen before. You will meet new adversaries who will cloud your true F.O.G. potential. You will hear their names on the media, al-Qaeda, Osama Bin-laden, anthrax, terrorism, panic, depression, cipro, and fear. But no matter how real they may seem, they have no real power compared to Operation F.O.G. For your words, thoughts, and actions will reflect Operation F.O.G. You will truly be asked to "love thy enemy" For in Operation F.O.G. you will come to see the enemy as aspects of yourself, crying out to be healed, only this time, on a much larger scale. So, when your friends and co-workers ask you, "what do you do in these times of uncertainty and fear?" You will simply reply, "I am in F.O.G." And remind them to FOCUS ON GOD.

In the past month we have all been deeply affected by the attacks on America. Some of us, myself included, have begun to question everything. They have made us reevaluate our lives and ourselves. What is it that I am wanting? Why do I feel so lonely? Whom do I need? Is there a point anymore? Why do I feel like going home and being with my family? What is my purpose? What is truly important too me?

I feel that the last two questions are perhaps the most difficult to answer and yet the most important. For is it possible that the recent tragedies upon our nation maybe a blessing in disguise? Perhaps they have stirred the inner most places of our being. Maybe the have forced us to ask question like "What is most important too me?" If you don't ask real questions you will never receive real answers. It is said that the answers are always there, when we stop avoiding the right questions. These events are asking us to go into the depths of our soul to question the very nature of our lives. "Who am I?" "What is it that I am truly wanting?" "What brings me joy, happiness, and peace?"

When President George W. Bush said, "They say that adversary introduces us to ourselves," he made a very powerful statement. I believe that the events on September 11, 2001, have forced to discover our most intimate self. THANK YOU GOD. They have forced us to ask questions. THANK YOU GOD. For most of us have been in hiding. The book of Genesis states,

"Adam, where are you? You are hiding from me" We have been hiding from our true nature for thousands of years. When Adam and Even ate from the "apple" of good and evil they created the mind-set of "perceived" separation from God. Your true, inner being knows the wonderful opportunity for you, which has been presented here. For you remember your connection to God more so then the others. For those who are caught up in the fear and chaos, they will look to you. They will want to know how you are peaceful and that they are not. ABC News recently reported that self-help and new age book sales are on the rise. (10/16/01) You the light-worker are needed. Now, more so than ever before. As a Jewish carpenter of long ago once said, "You are the light of the world."

For there will come a time in the not so distant future when the public will no longer look to our Government for answers. Rather, they will turn to you. They will call upon you for answers. They will seek you out and they too will see your light. They will know that you have something that they want. "For if you drink of this water you shall thirst no more" As you drink from the "water" of your soul "holy spirit" "inner being" you shall no longer feel separate from God. You will no longer be in thirst. (For you are literally thirsting for God)

As you come out of your own hiding, you will automatically liberate others from their own hiding. Yes, they will seek you out. These are the times. This is your moment of glory. This is what you came here to do, to "set the captives free." Now, is your opportunity, what are you waiting for? Live your dreams, live your life to the utmost, dream the impossible dream, and make it so.

10

What does God and our Angels want?

I am asked many times, "what do you think that God and our Angels wants from us?" Often I reply, "I am not sure, but I think that God and our Angels wants to be admired, honored, valued, acknowledged, respected, cherished, appreciated, and loved." Then I continue by stating, "I would guess that they want all of the things that we most want." After all, didn't God create us in his/her likeness and in his/her image? I recall one weekend afternoon I was ranting and raving to God about how my girlfriend didn't appreciate me and didn't really honor anything that I did for her. I deeply felt that she would always find ways to put me down for not being absolutely perfect. I continued to complain about my relationship with her, when God said, "Do you really treat *yourself* any differently?" I said, "what?" God again replied, "Do you really treat *yourself* any differently?" I had to take a step back and realize that God was right. I stopped and I had to look at all of the ways that I did not appreciate myself. How I did not value or honor my gifts. How I was overly critical of myself. How I was not very kind or gentle to myself. Needless to say it was a real eye opener. Yet, is this not the dynamics of personal relationships? Do we not get to see all aspects of ourselves when we have another who is our mirror for us? Do they not reflect back to us where we have been most wounded? Do they not enable us to see how we feel about ourselves in the moment? Is life not an absolute reflection of you? So, if you want a new reflection then you must change how you truly feel about yourself. So, if we really want to know what it is that God is most wanting for us? It must be to accept the absolute perfection of its manifestation that is called you. This begins when you are willing to accept the love that your inner being has for you. It is about creating an intimate relationship with your soul. For it is here where you will find inner perfection.

OK, Mr. Mark Clinton Patterson, all of this sounds great, and maybe you are able to do this, but how do *I* create a relationship from within? How do I come to a place where I can trust my inner being? How do even know that my soul or inner being exists? Where do I find my passion? How do I know what it is that I am truly, truly wanting? Start by being quiet. The language of God is silence. I recall a dream that I had where I was on the Larry King live talk show. He asked me, "So, do you really believe that you have discovered the Kingdom of Heaven that is within you?" I replied, "Yes, Larry, I have. Does this mean that I have mastered it? Absolutely, not."

How do you know that you have an inner being or a soul? Well, the Church has gone out of its way in trying to convince you that it is damned to Hell for eternity if you don't believe in a certain way. But how do you really know? Right now what is it that is enabling you to read these words? What is it that enables you to hear a conversation? Some of you might argue that it is your mind? I would say that your mind is telling you whether to believe any of the words that are written on these pages or not? What is it that enables you to feel that something is not right when someone is telling you a lie? Yes, this is your inner being or your soul. So, how do you develop a relationship with it? Well, how do you develop a relationship with anything else? Acknowledge it. Ask it to reveal too you what it is that you are truly wanting. Introduce yourself to it. Say, "Hello soul, I need to **listen** too you. You see my friend I have allowed my mind to make some mistakes in my life. So, I am asking to see if you can guide me on the path that I intended before I came here? Soul, inner-self, I have a hard time trusting. So, can we start with small things first? Like, if I ask you to remind me things that bring me joy, and if they come to me in a dream, or if someone mentions it in a passing conversation, then I'll know that you are speaking to me." One of the most powerful things that you can ask your soul to reveal too you is this, "Inner being please reveal to me what it is that I am *feeling* about myself that is producing this quality of life that I am not wanting." You can also ask, "Inner being what is the image of my self that I am holding at this time?" You can also ask, "Inner being, what action do I need to take in the physical that will help me heal my self image?"

Once you begin to ask questions of your inner being, the answers will come. You will probably not like the answers but they will be revealed too you. What is really exciting is that once you start to ask question, you will intuitively get more questions to ask. As you learn to trust this process, then you can take the next step. Ask your inner being to enable you to feel the love, but only to the ability that you can handle it, that it has for you. Once you begin to feel this then use this feeling in your meditation. Close your eyes and in your inner mind as to feel the love that your soul has for you. Allow that feeling to expand. Allow it to encompass your entire being. As you are doing this, begin to breathe in and out of your heart area. As you are breathing in and out of your heart area. (You do this by simply moving energy through your heart area) You call out in your inner mind; "I love God." "I love me." "I am loved." "I am good." Repeat these phrases often. Allow the feeling of love from within to become even greater. As you practice this, you may even begin to feel or hear a song or a melody. This is the music of your inner being. Many people refer to this as bliss or joy. This is the nectar of your soul. This is what your life force is thirsting for. This is the one thing in life that you will never have to worry about running out of. For its supply is limitless. As you allow yourself to feel this song, it will open your heart to God. You will experience the love, the adoration, and the joy that your soul truly has for you. A love that is based on no conditions, no expectations, no tests, and it has no expense. This is where you will learn to absolutely feel good about yourself regardless of where you are at in any given moment. There is not a greater gift that you can give to yourself then the feeling of self worth. As you allow your feeling of self worth to grow your life will reflect this back too you one hundred fold. You will understand what Jesus meant when he said, "It is God's good pleasure to grant you the kingdom." You will be liberated and know that you are a child of the utmost high. You will become a beacon of light in a dark world. As Nelson Mandella stated when he quoted Marianne Williamson, "as you allow your light to shine, you automatically give others permission to do the same." Yes, dear child, this is what God is most wanting, to grant you the keys to the kingdom. Just remember that the kingdom is right here today and now. There is not a greater opportunity to experience it, then while you are in the physical body. What are you waiting for? Embrace the love that comes from within you that is for you. Acknowledge that you are worth more and that you deserve the best that life has to offer. In doing so, you will become that child of the utmost high and be free at last. (I would guess that the one thing that we probably need to be most freed from is our hang-ups around sexuality)

11

Placing Spirituality back into our Sexuality
Spiritual Orgasms

Spiritual what? Orgasms! Yes, Spiritual Orgasms! "When we have restored the sexual experience to the realm of the sacred, our world will be chaste, divine, holy and healed," says Deepak Chopra, MD I cannot think of anything that needs healing more than our own sexuality. Why is there so much confusion around sexuality? Why do we have sexually transmitted diseases? HIV/AIDS? Why have we been taught that sexuality is bad, dirty, and sinful, yet it feels so good? What about masturbation? I haven't gone blind or developed hair on my palms, and it always feels good and it brings me a lot of pleasure. If sexuality is innate and that desire comes from deep within, how can it be bad or shameful? If it comes from within, how can a gay or lesbian individual be immoral or wrong? How can homosexuality be a genetic defect?

From the point of view of genetics, we are all bisexual. Recently, science has shown that half of our genes are received from the male and half from the female. Why is it that if two beautiful, curvaceous women make love, society says its okay? Yet if two attractive, well-endowed men have sex, that same society turns around and utters its disgust?

Why is it that when a man sleeps with hundreds of women, he is called a stud? Yet, if a female sleeps with hundreds of men, she is called a slut or a whore? Does the act of sex in and of itself cause disease, or are there other factors?

What can we do to restore the sexual experience to the realm of the sacred and divine? What if one of the purposes of the orgasm is to help you connect directly into your soul?

French philosopher and mathematician Renee Descartes argued that consciousness was contained within the pineal gland. The pineal glad is an endocrine gland that is smaller than a quarter and located directly behind the center of your forehead. It is often referred to as the "master gland." I believe that if the pineal glad is activated directly, it will lead to altered states of consciousness, enabling you to become like the Christ. There is no greater way to activate Christ-Consciousness then by activating the pineal gland via an orgasm.

In Sanskrit, the ancient language of India, the word "chakra" refers to energy centers, or vortexes, in the body. These wheels of energy are located within the etheric or astral body and relate to various aspects of both mental and physical health.

There are seven chakras. The first chakra—the root chakra—is located at the base of your spine. It is red in color and relates to sexuality and the sense of survival. The next chakra is the spleen chakra. Its color is orange and it relates to mobility in life. It is located between the etheric or astral body and relate to various aspects of both mental and physical health. The sixth is your third-eye chakra. Its color is indigo and it relates to your intuition and ability to trust yourself. It is located in the center of your forehead. Seventh is the crown chakra. Its color is a white and purple mixture; it relates to your God self or Higher self. This chakra is located at the top of your head.

When these wheels of energy are energized and balanced, you will feel energized and charged with vitality. When they are blocked due to emotionally charged imprints, they can cause illness and disease. So, what do these chakras have to do with sex, orgasm, the pineal gland, and the ability to achieve Christ-consciousness? In one word, *everything*.

Recently, I attended an evening with Deepak Chopra, M.D. interestingly enough; one-third of that evening was focused on the human orgasm. Now, how many of you have ever noticed where your orgasm goes internally? How many of you on achieving an orgasm finds your self dizzy, or you feel like you are "out of your mind!" In Sanskrit sexual energy is called "Kundalini." In Taoism it is called "Chi" or "Qi" which means life energy. In Vedic traditions it is called "Parana" meaning life force. If you were to pay attention to your orgasm internally, you would notice that it does in fact move towards the pineal gland. Does it go all of the way to the top of your head? I would guess that for most of you, it stops somewhere between your navel and your throat chakra. Unfortunately, in men the sexual energy gets stuck in the solar plexuses and in women it is stuck in the throat area.

In many of the above mentioned eastern teachings sexuality can be used to open consciousness and access realms of the siddih's (or enlightened ones) Stop and think about the Christian Cross and the Egyptian Auhnk. Two religious symbols with different meanings. The Christian Cross represents "The Resurrection," while the Auhnk symbolizes "Immortality."

Now, historically speaking the Egyptian Auhnk existed for thousands of years before the Cross. Was the Auhnk a representation of what was possible? Were we meant to be "immortal?" (If you recall the story of Adam and Eve, God never said that we couldn't eat from the fruit of immortality.) Instead of viewing these two symbols as "religious" think of them as the way "sexual energy" can flow in the body. For an example imagine the Christian Cross, and imagine that as you orgasm, the "Chi" flows in the way of the cross up then down then out both sides and the orgasm just leaves the "body." Are you following this?

Now think about the Egyptian Auhnk. What happens? Yes, that is right! The circular top of the Auhnk allows the "Chi" or sexual orgasm to flow back into the body. It is re-circulated, it never gets lost. What a concept! Using sexual energy to "re-charge" the body! In tantric sex, this is what they teach men to do. "Creating an inner Auhnk," via sexual energy.

If you learn how to do this, you will create "inner-bliss" and your partner will love you for it. Let's say that you are getting ready to climax, and instead of ejaculating "outward," you learned to ejaculate "inward." What if you used control and directed the flow of the semen towards the pineal gland? You can do this by using your lower abdominal muscles. As you begin to reach climax take the orgasm pull your muscle contraction upward/inward and move it up your spine and into the center of the forehead. Relax, wait a few minutes until you are in "control" and repeat the process several times. This over time can create a state of "oneness" In your state of "oneness" all fears, pain, judgements would be resolved. Eventually you would become aware of who you really are.

Now, if you saw the movie, "Something about Mary," the character "Ben?" was given advice before his date with Mary, right? To masturbate.... Why? Because it is true.... when we climax externally, our right brain and left-brain hemispheres become in sync with each other. We become open, vulnerable, and we let go of all of our defenses. As we orgasm we surrender completely. Our mind is on the path of least resistance. We become more aware of our inner being. And this is exactly what Dr. Chopra spoke of when he said; "The Orgasm is what leads us to our intimate connection to the God or the Christ that is within us."

As you know, I had Near Death Experience 16 years ago, and YES there are Angels, and they are absolutely envious of our ability to ORGASM. Although, they point out that we have yet learned how to truly master our sexuality and orgasms in achieving "higher states" of consciousness.

Why can sex be solely for procreation? In my opinion women have the right not to bring children into this world. Your sexuality and ability to orgasm is your vehicle to becoming one with God. Why does the church make sexuality so sinful? Why does the church make homosexuality wrong? Why does the church make sex so shameful? What is the reason behind this suppression? Why does the church claim that the sole reason for sexuality is procreation? There can be only one reason—to keep you from re-membering who you really are. Unfortunately, most of our guilt, fear, and shame has been placed right between our legs by the church.

And this in my opinion, is why the Catholic and Judeo-Christian churches taught people that sex was "sinful and bad." Now stop and think about this. If you could become "Christ like" or "Buddha like" via sexuality, then they could not control you through their guilt, shame, and fear programs. Because if you achieved the atonement ("at-one-ment") then you wouldn't you need to be "saved" nor would you need a "savior." You would free yourself from them. You would be FREE!

The Catholic Church went to such an extent to suppress sexuality that it still refers to Mary as a virgin. Again, 2,000, years ago in the Middle East, the term "virgin" did not mean, "not having sexual experience." It meant, "not being attached to any man." The term was quite often reserved for temple prostitutes who initiated young males into adulthood. It is interesting to note that 2,000 years ago in the Middle East; a young woman was often referred to as a "Virgo." Don't you think that it is quite possible that the term "Virgo" got translated into "virgin"? I certainly do. Mary certainly did not remain a virgin all of her life. As it is documented that she and Joseph did bear other children.

So, when you have sex with someone, make it sacred. Make it a ritual for the soul. Take the time to invoke the inner Christ, the light that is within each of you. Take the time to light candles and honor each other. Take the time to gaze deeply into each other's eyes and connect with each other's souls. Make kissing such a powerful act that it becomes more erotic than the act of sex itself. Touch. Take the time to touch, hold and caress.

It is really sad that in today's society, we only know two types of touching—sexual and violence. When you hold and touch your partner, do it with love. Allow love to flow from your soul out to your fingertips. Allow your touch to become soft, gentle and nurturing. When you touch your partner, look at her and tell her you love her. Be willing to work with the body's energy centers and allow the sexual pulse to flow into each of the chakras and up towards the pineal gland. Allow the experience of orgasm to enter the realm of the sacred once again.

12

What is your relationship with God?

Here is a question that you would expect a TV minister to ask. What is your relationship with God? They will also try to convince you that your relationship with God can only come through knowing and accepting Jesus. Well, I think that there is a better way for one to determine where their relationship with God is? I would guess that your relationship with your parents is probably a good indicator of where your relationship with God/Goddess is. Are they not representations of your heavenly mother and father? If you feel that your father has abandoned you, then I would guess that you probably feel that God has as well. Do you feel that your father hasn't done enough for you? Well, you probably feel that God hasn't either. Do you feel that your father doesn't listen to you or understand you? Maybe you feel the same about God? Maybe another way to look at this, is to consider that you choose your parents to reflect back too you, where you are at with God in any given moment. Do you feel that your mother doesn't love you? Do you feel the same about Goddess? Do you not trust your mother or your father? Do you trust God? Do you recall a time in your childhood when you would take your father's hand and in doing so, you felt that you could do *anything*? When you were holding your dad's hand as a young toddler, didn't you feel that with him, you could go anywhere? Did you not ask for your father's hand as a child so that you could feel safe, protected, and loved? As long as you were hand and hand with your father's was there any fear of exploring, finding new friends, or trying new things? As a child you trusted in the power of your father. And is this not true, when we are willing to hold the hand of God and trust in it, do we not feel safe? Do we not become more secure, more powerful? Do you not believe that you will be protected no matter what you do? Do you hear what I am getting at? As you heal your relationship with your father and mother you will once again heal your relationship with God/Goddess. You will be willing to take their hand and allow yourself to fully trust, surrender, and have faith. As you heal your relationship with your physical parents you heal your relationship with God.

I know some of you are asking, "what if my father raped me?" If this is the case then you must be willing to consider that you made a contract or an agreement with your father because you were the one who violated him in a previous incarnation. So, our opportunity here is forgiveness. There are only opportunities to learn forgiveness. You may also want to look at the ways that you believe that God is either punishing you or betraying you. Did you feel that your father was with holding from you or that he owed you? When Jesus was speaking about removing the poisons from the pig, he was talking about clearing out the anger, rage, and resentment that we often feel towards whom have hurt us. Now, that I have addressed our relationship with our physical father's as reflections of our relationship to our father God, I would like to disclose my own relationship to mine.

In the early 90's Fortune 500 CEO's were asked, "What is the most impressive thing that you look for on a resume?" The overwhelming response to this question was "An Eagle Scout." As they felt that the honor of an Eagle Scout represented, loyalty, determination, courage, leadership, honesty, integrity, and commitment. My father was an Eagle Scout. Less than 2 percent of all boy scouts make Eagle Scout. Unfortunately, he was also manic depressant, paranoid schizophrenic, psychotic, and required heavy medication for most of his life. My mother divorced my father before my third birthday. He was 32 and went back home to live with his parents where he has remained his adult life. Even today, he still lives in his parent's home, alone. My grandparents passed away in 1996 and 1997. My father was also a born again Christian. Not only was he born again, he became evangelic. He is a true bible thumper. He has every word, every scripture, every passage memorized in his mind. Yet, he was filled with self-condemnation, self-loathing, guilt, resentment, and unworthiness. So, the idea that *only* Jesus was worthy to receive God's love matched his beliefs about himself. He was convinced that he was a no good sinner filled with sin and his only redemption was a personal savior, Jesus Christ. Despite all of his faith in Jesus, despite sending thousands of dollars to Pat Robertson, Jimmy Swaggert, and Oral Roberts, my father still condemns himself to this day as a complete failure as a man and especially as a husband. My father never remarried and to my knowledge he never dated anyone after he and my mother divorced.

As a child, I would look forward to seeing my father. We would have walks at the park in the small town of Allerton, Iowa. We loved to shoot the B-B gun and the Bow and Arrow. We played catch with the baseball in the front yard. We would go swimming and Lake Red Rock in Chariton, Iowa. He would play the piano and sing gospel songs. Often, he would come and pick me up in Iowa City, Iowa, and then he would drive me three hours to Allerton. Often we would stop in Oskaloosa to eat lunch. He would slap me on the knee and say, "Mark old buddy of mine, boy I am glad that you are with me." On the way there we would make up songs for fun, to make the time pass. "Grandpa, Grandpa, going so slow, you think that you are going so fast, but you really need to give it more gas…" Yes, this was one of our favorites. He had a way about musical rhymes. He was always making jingles up that usually made no sense at all, they were just silly. Yes, we had a lot of laughs. Then I was about 10-11 years old. We were at a Dairy Queen in Iowa City, Iowa. My father froze. He began to drool. His hands began to shake, tremble uncontrollably. People started to stare at him, at us. At that moment I became painfully aware of my father's condition. Finally he snapped out of it. He said, "Mark, I am so sorry Mark, so sorry." We left the DQ then over to my house and where my cousin Shawn and some of our friends were waiting for us to return. We were all playing and laughing and I recall them feeling that my dad, was OK, that he was funny. I couldn't help but think of the incident that took place just an hour ago. I was praying to God that he would just go home. I prayed to God that he wasn't really my father. I began to fantasize that he was not my father. I hated everything about him. I hated that he constantly smoked, constantly preached, constantly paced back and forth, and that he lived at home with his parents. I did not want anything to do with him. As the summer sun began to set, he went back home to Allerton, and I went to my bedroom crying. I resented him to the core of my being. As the years passed visits to Allerton, Iowa, became less frequent. The ones that were made lasted only a couple of days. When I turned 16, I would drive down myself only to spend a couple of hours with him. I would go, say hello, and then turn right around and drive back. I couldn't wait to get out of that smoke filled house. By the time I was 19 I was fully into the New Age philosophy. In 1989, I went to Sedona, Arizona, a new age mecca. I felt that I was in Heaven. In 1990, I attended a psychic seminar with Dick Sutphen that was also in Sedona. The following year I attended another Sutphen seminar in Chicago, Illinois. Dick Sutphen is a best selling author, past life hypnotist, and considered one of America's fore most psychic researcher. I became fascinated with past lives and past life regression. I felt so strongly that I could use the techniques that I was shown in the seminars; I began to practice on my friends. I found that I was a natural at placing people in a hypnotic state. My friends were experiencing vivid details of previous lifetimes and the results were amazing. I began to study more about psychic phenomenon, reincarnation, ESP; UFO's the whole New Age bit. I loved all of it and I could not get enough. My father was convinced that one of these days I was going to see the light. I on the other hand, kept informing him that I had already been to the light. He was convinced that Satan himself created my near death experience, and that I had not gone to Heaven. He told me that he prayed for me every night that I would go to the right God, his God. In 1993, I moved to Charleston, SC, and my father and I began some of our most intense debates over religion. I recall on afternoon when my father said, "Mark you are right, Christianity does have its faults." I could not believe my ears when he said it. I actually felt for a moment that he might be listening to me that he might be trying to understand me. Then he would turn around and proclaim, "Mark, Jesus is the only way." I cannot tell you how many times I would slam the phone on him cursing his "foolishness." I would get so mad at him. At a core level of my being I felt that he did not understand me. Boy, I was bound and determined to make him understand me. The only problem was that he was just as bound and determined to make me understand him. Round and round we would go. We would both spouted off quotes from the scriptures, psalms, versus, and parables. We would both put our interpretations of them and we would just end up getting nowhere. I would point out historical facts around the teachings of reincarnation. He would not listen to any of the documented facts and just proclaim, "Jesus, Jesus, and Jesus." Then I would scream, "If Jesus is such a healer, why hasn't he delivered you from your mental illness?" "Yeah that's right, take the cross and shove it up your a**!" But no matter how many times I hung up on him. No matter how many times I told him where to stick Jesus, and the cross, he still loved me. No matter what I did, believed, or said, my father loved me. One night my father informed me that it was always his dream for me to become the next Oral Roberts. I was quick to reply, "Be careful for what you wish for, it may come true. You may not like what I am preaching, but as God as my witness, I will create a nationally syndicated TV ministry."

So, Back and forth we would go in our attempts to make each other understand. Years went on and by this time I had been living in Las Cruces, New Mexico. My feelings that he didn't do enough for me, and that he owed me were still rampant in my anger towards him. These feelings of resentment towards him became so great that I betrayed my father. And despite my betrayal against him, he still forgave me. He still loved me. Isn't this the downfall of humanity? We constantly reject the love that God is giving to us. My rejection of my father's loves became symbolic of my unwillingness to accept the love that God has for me. My father still believed in me. And isn't this true about God? No matter what we do, God will still wait for us. God will still be there. God love for us will always be there. God is merely waiting for us to claim it as ours. Don't worry that love will still be there for you. God's love has no conditions. It is patient. Quietly waiting for you to be still enough to feel it.

It is like Walter Starke of the "Now Age" says, "You can commit a sin against the father and be forgiven. You can commit a sin against the son and be forgiven. When you commit a sin against the Holy Spirit that is what is unforgivable." I think that he is referring to the idea that "sin" is betraying ourselves. Or like I have stated, "not being true to our inner being."

It was also during this time that I dreamt that my father was in a prison cell. In his prison cell I started kicking him, hitting him, and literally beating him up. I was relentless. Then in my dream my father turned into me. That is when I realized that in keeping my father in "prison" with hatred, I was only doing harm to myself. I woke up from that dream realizing what I was doing. I woke up from that dream having a feeling of compassion for my father. I had a compassion for my father that I had never experienced before. I no longer wanted to make him understand me. I no longer wanted to make him wrong. I wanted to understand him. I wanted to heal our relationship and it took me committing an act of betrayal against him to do it. You see God has a way of making the "wrong" actions of man "right." In the book of Daniel, Daniel was a man who prospered. He was able to produce incredible harvest. It was said that Daniel was a man of integrity. The Hebrew meaning of prosperity means integrity. To be prosperous must one be of integrity. And prosper Daniel did. He was gifted and talented and was well liked in his community. He also had a couple of brothers who were very envious of him.

They were not happy that their father played favorites with Daniel. Eventually, Daniel was wrongly sent to prison by his jealous brothers. Even though he was sent to prison he became a leader. The guards became aware of his ability to lead others. He was given special treatment and was looked up to by those in prison. Daniel was let out of prison, only to be betrayed by his brothers once again. Soon Daniel found himself as a slave. But his character was strong and people took notice. He taught the slave owners how to store food for the lean times ahead. He became a leader amongst the other slaves. The years passed on and eventually Daniel's brother's ended up into slavery since they lost the good fortune that was given to them by their father. Although they did not recognize Daniel, Daniel recognized them. The brothers went on their knees when Daniel welcomed them with open arms. Daniel forgave them. Daniel was eventually released and was given a large amount of land. Why? God corrected the wrong actions of Daniel's brothers. God corrected my actions against my father. My crime against my father brought us closer together. It brought us closer together because my father, loved me, believed in me, and forgave me. In doing so, I began to believe in him. I began to love him. I began to see that he truly did love me. We began to heal our relationship. I also realized that my action was a crying out for his love. Aren't we all crying out to receive God's love in one way or another? It is said that everything that we do is either an act of love, or crying out for it.

My father forgave me because he believed in me. He believed in me because of his unwavering love for me. In the past few months we have become very close. We now have meaningful conversations. I know that he gave me everything that he had. We are making peace with each other. As I heal my relationship with my physical father, my connection God, the heavenly father, has become clearer, stronger, and more secure. So, I have come to know that God believes in me, because I know a father, that believes is me. Thank you God.

Forty-five years of chain smoking have finally taken their toll on my father. Tomorrow is Tuesday November 27, 2001, and he is headed for the VA hospital in Des Moines, Iowa. He has all of the signs of having 3 mild heart attacks which is usually the precursor to a major heart attack. So, I have said all of the things that I needed to say to him. We are closer than ever before. I listen to my father without the need or desire to make him understand me. He no longer feels that I don't listen to him. He feels that I understand him. It is great. God truly does correct the wrong actions of man.

Thank you God. Dear people, if you knew that you only had one hour to live, whom would you call and what would you say? If you know the answer to these two questions, what are you waiting for?

13

How can you ascend into Heaven if you keep nailing yourself to the Cross?

Jesus said, "Judge not that yea be judged. For the judgement that you have shall be the judgement that you get. The measure that you give shall be the measure that you will receive." "Judge not that yea be judged." Clearly Jesus states here that we are NOT judged by God. Judge not that you are judged. However, your judgments of others will be how you are judged. And what you give out in life is what you will get back. (KARMA) If God is LOVE, then LOVE by it's nature, cannot judge. LOVE can only heal, forgive, allow, and expand us into who we really are. Yet, we are in a constant state of Judgement about each other and especially ourselves. You judge yourself more than anyone else could. With all of the would of, could of, and should of's. All of the not enough's, self-condemnation, not smart enough etc, and how could God possibly judge you? You have already judged yourself as being "guilty" Yet Jesus said, "Judge NO ONE for you do not know how they stand in the eyes of God." Well, wouldn't this same principal apply too you? When Jesus was with Mary Magdalene it is quoted that he said, "Let he who is without sin, cast the first stone." In my opinion, what he actually said was, "Let he who has not laid with her, cast the first stone." Then he said to her, paraphrasing (The love that you have offered me today casts away all of your sins, go forth and sin no more.)

Now, this is important, because first, he wasn't referring to the love that she offered him Jesus the man, she was referring to the love that she offered to God. Second, "sin" means missing the mark of your soul's purpose. So, he was asking her to follow the path of your soul. When you realize that the love that you are capable of giving to "God" is greater than missing the mark of your life, then you can go forward and create a life that is based on the mark of your purpose.

Unfortunately, we keep ourselves nailed to the cross, by believing that we are unworthy, guilty, thus undeserving, of a second, third, fourth, fifth, unlimited, chances to follow the mark of our soul. When Jesus said, "I am here to set the captives free" He was sent here to show what was possible when you took your self off the cross "resurrection" and follow the path of the soul. You are the beloved child of God. You have never, never, done anything wrong. You have merely missed the mark of your purpose. The love that you have offered God is far greater than this. As Edgar Cayce said, "The laws of grace supercede the laws of karma." So, stop crucifying yourself, for you are a child of God with whom S/he is most pleased!

14

The Violet Flame of Forgiveness

I truly believe in my heart of hearts that it all boils down to forgiveness. Forgiveness means to forego the pain that we hold onto when we feel that another has hurt us or betrayed us. It also means forgoing the pain that we inflict upon ourselves when we believe that we are unworthy, pathetic, and not smart enough, a disappointment, or that we haven't don't enough. It is about forgoing the need to make decisions that are based on our emotionally charged imprints that are contained in our energy field. It is about forgoing the belief that we have done only wrong in our lives. It is about forgoing our mistakes and thus correcting them. As you learn to forego pain and express only love a deepening takes place. You begin to realize that no one including yourself has ever done anything wrong. You are lead to the place of knowing that there is nothing to forgive. You come to know that there is only an absence of love. There has only been an absence of self-love. When you hold onto pain, and the need to be right that the other has "wronged" you, the only person who you are harming is yourself. When you hold onto the pain of anger, resentment, fear, blame, envy, or jealousy you are creating dis-ease. You are not at ease with your natural state of love. Who you are is love. When you allow that natural state of love to expand itself from within, your life will change. Your life will become miraculous. Your every thought, every action, every spoken word will reflect God. So, how do you get there? How does one reach complete self-forgiveness? In my opinion one of the most powerful tools for self-forgiveness is the meditation called, "Invoking the violet flame of forgiveness." The following is taken with permission from anextstep.org

Invoking the Violet Flame of Forgiveness

Breath Meditation for most Westerners has been an elusive partner. Try as many do, the chatterbox (monkey mind, inner dialogue) seems to control even the highest intentioned "sit". The purpose of the "sit" is to shut out the world to create a place of quiet within; to commune with the Higher Self.

Many of us in the West haven't had the training in any form of yoga or meditation. Because it has not been a part of our upbringing or culture, we lack the discipline to quiet our mind. As a result we tend to live in constant noise (inside and out of our heads), which creates perpetual sensory overload-emotionally, mentally and physically. This disallows clarity and ease of being in our creative and spiritual process. It also drives us forward into the future or buries us in the past.

Introducing a conscious breath into meditation helps us being/staying present. It centers us and supports us in relaxing our physiology. We are able to reach calm. We are able to let go. When we create this experience time ceases to be. Everything troublesome ceases to be. Bursting the Body Light-Violet Flame of Forgiveness accomplishes this and much more.

The breath meditations that are Bursting the Body Light-Violet Flame of Forgiveness are unlike other breath meditations. They have been given by Source at this specific time to spiritually advance us. These breath meditations stand apart because they have extra healing power...a power we have not been ready to receive before. They are loving dispensation to a birthright we have not wanted to claim. You are ready now or you wouldn't be reading this.

The Bursting the Body Light-the violet flame of forgiveness breath/meditation is a building process. It is vitally important that you follow the directions as given, gradually adding breath sets. This is not Rebirthing or Conscious Energy Breathwork, this is very different. We ask that you respect yourself enough to follow the instructions. Your breath-life force is exquisitely connected to your Light Body. It is of utmost importance that you do this gently, compassionately and slowly. Read the instructions through a few times before you begin.

*****Please note: Should you start feeling tension or tingling in your mouth, face, hands, body, recognize that your body is releasing long held tension-pain. It is called tetany and is a good thing! Relax, reduce the breathing process at the level you're at; breathe easy, long breaths—your body will release the tightness and then you can continue.*****

This breath/meditation process is to be done at least once a day because that is the only way it will work! It will take 10-15 minutes or longer if you choose. It may be done as many as two or three times a day and no more than three times a day. Remember this is about expanding compassion for yourself and others. Be gentle with yourself. This is not a race. You have plenty of time. It is imperative that you take the time to gradually build with this first breath/meditation.

You want to love your Light Body, being gentle with it and with yourself. The Bursting the Body Light breath/Violet flame of forgiveness meditation is not a replacement for your current path-work or tools. It is an enhancement to your over all process. Incorporate it into your present discipline.

You will definitely be aware of an increase of potency or capability in your tools and yourself, especially if you are doing this three times a day. Please put space of at least an hour between each Bursting the Body Light breath/meditation. You may want to keep a journal to pen your experiences, you may not. Know that God-Goddess loves you and are closer than each breath you take.

Part 1-Bursting the Body Light-The Cleanse Breath Meditation As you read this make certain you are taking relaxed, full, complete breaths. Keep reminding your body to let go. Find a quiet location, free of distraction. You may sit or lie down. During this exercise your body may cool and this is okay. You may want to cover yourself. It is also okay to do this with eyes open or closed. Mudra: Hand Placement. Place all fingertips together gently-baby finger to baby finger, thumb-to-thumb, etc. Do not exert pressure while doing this. Hold this mudra (your hands) as in prayer fashion in front of chest or in your lap. Maintain the mudra the whole time (through the breath sets). Breath use: You may use either mouth or nose breathing. Your eyes may be open or closed.

There are two parts to the breath, together they constitute one set. 1st part: Breathe into your abdomen with short, full, connected breaths (no pause be-tween inhalation and exhalation). Each inhale and exhale equals one breath. Do 12 short breaths (not quick, not panting). Make certain your belly is rising and falling with each breath. Pull the inhalation in, relax the exhalation out. Do not push or blow out the exhalation.

You may not be practiced at breathing into your abdomen. It will feel good. Then immediately. 2nd part: Breathe into your heart with long, full-connected breaths. Make certain your rib cage and shoulders are moving with each of these breaths. Each inhale and exhale equals one breath. Pull the inhalation in, relax the exhalation out. Do not push or blow out the exhalation. Do 5 of these long breaths. The twelve breaths to the abdomen and five to the chest equals one set. The short breaths (12) of the exercise are not rapid, nor panting; they are short, even, full, relaxed. The long breaths (5) are generous and very full-in a relaxed body. The twelve long and five short breaths make one set.

The beginning number of sets is six and you will gradually add sets as per the following instructions: Day one, two and three,—do six sets. Day four, five and six,—do nine sets. Day seven, eight and nine,—do twelve sets. (Continue doing 12 sets until you choose to begin part 2-the Violet Flame of Forgiveness). Cleanse: Upon completion of the breaths, with your conscious intention, open the minor chakras on the bottom of your feet and the palms of your hands.

Visualize this happening or simply allow it. Decide what aspects of God-Goddess (i.e. Jesus, Mother/Father God, Babaji, Wankan Tanka, Mother Mary, Earth Mother, Yahweh, Allah etc. [They are all the same]) or Teachers, Guides, Guardians, Allies you wish to invoke for support in cleansing out of your bodies the energy that feels heavy, dark, stagnant, obstructed or allow Mother Father God to handle this for you. Invoke those you wish, as you open your crown (top of head). Allow them to quickly or slowly move out what needs moving out through your hands and/or your feet.

When you feel done, close the minor chakras of your hands and feet and the crown. Give thanks to those who offered love and support. You may end this session here or you may use this energy to meditate for as long as you desire. RELAX, BREATHE, ALLOW YOURSELF TO BE THE EXPERIENCE! It is imperative that you take the time to gradually build with this first breath/medita-tion. You want to love your Light Body, being gentle with it and with yourself. Congratulations!

We knew you could do it. We are excited for you. Mother Earth is enthusiastic about your participation in Lighting up the Earth to its intended capacity of Conscious Awareness. You are now ready to acquire the 2nd part of Bursting the Body Light—which is the Violet Flame of Forgiveness breath/meditation. You will be acquiring through donation the 15 page text of both The Cleanse Part I and the Violet Flame of Forgiveness Part II of Bursting the Body Light and their procedures. This text will answer your questions on this subject and more. You will also receive gratis, the ebook Free-Ways to Higher Consciousness Volume I. In addition, you will receive gratis our monthly newsletter "Tools to Higher Consciousness" if you have not already signed up for it.

I encourage all of you to look into the second part of this mediation. It will enable you to create a more loving relationship with your self. Your light body will expand immensely. Mine went from a 10% activation to a 98% activation in less than a month using both parts of this breath work. In doing this meditation you feel an intimate connection to God, you will become more at peace and create greater harmony in your life. As you create harmony with God/Goddess you will feel guided, you will know that you are at the right place at the right time. You will see miracles become the story of your life. You will see God in all things that you do. You will have a new spirit that soars with the Eagles. You will live life with awe. In invoking the violet flame of forgiveness you will cry out, "I love God." Your heart will experience a love from the self and for the self that you cannot fathom. You will become the divine aspect of God expressing itself through you as you. You will know that God believes in you, because you will believe in yourself. You will become the miracle and that my friend is just how your life will work. Because you will understand that that is just the way your is. And so it is.

15

That is just the story of my Life

Friends, without question, I live a charmed life. I am guided and I walk hand and hand with God. At the core of my being I know that I am one of her messengers. I have been taken to the Promised Land I have heard the harpsichords of the Angels. I have heard the Celestial Choir and I have heard a music that changed my life forever. It brought me to my knees. I believe that I am always at the right place at the right time. Whatever I ask for I am given and that is the story of my life. I am a channel for the light and an instrument of the divine. This is just the way my life works. I know that it can be the same for you. It can become the same for you due to this simple little tool that I am going to share with you. (This is adapted from the 15-minute miracle)

I want for you a time to recall in your life when you felt something fell into place without much effort. An example would be like when I asked God for a place to stay and my friend Darianne called me later that evening to inform me of a room that was available. As you recall an event in your life that was "synchronistic" begin to expand on those feelings of amazement, awe, and gratitude. Recall what it was like when you could not believe that it happened so effortlessly. Then as the feeling of excitement about what happened continues to expand, state in your inner mind, "That is just the story of my life!" Or you can say it like this, "That is just the way my life is." Now, stop and think about something that it is that you are wanting. Let's say that you want to go to Hawaii. First create or remember those feelings of "synchronicity" and begin to allow them to expand. Then state something like, "You know I always receive plane tickets, and there is always someone who is able to connect me with someone that I can stay with, and I just always have enough money on my vacations. I just seem to be able to make the right connections to make things happen in my life. And that is just the way my life works. That is the story of my life!" Be willing to expand the feeling of "That is the story of my life!" Really feel with joy, "That's just the way my life works." Do this with a group of people who support you and believe in you and watch what happens. Now, you can apply this to anything that you want. Just be prepared...and expect miracles. Follow your bliss, do things that create joy in your life. Do things that create aliveness and passion within you. Be passionate about yourself and your work. Do things that increase your life force, rather than things and relationships that deplete it. Joy, passion, enthusiasm, and a sincere appreciation for life, is what will make life worth living. They will lead you to self-actualization. You will live a charmed life. You will be considered a deliberate creator. When people ask you, "Why is your life so amazing?" You will respond with a sparkle in your eye, "The Universe is good to me, the universe is so good to me, God is good to me, and God believes in me, and that is the story of my life."

0-595-26909-5